THE BOOK OF
PIZZAS
AND ITALIAN BREADS

T H E   B O O K   O F

PIZZAS
AND ITALIAN BREADS

SARAH BUSH

Photographed by
JON STEWART

a Salamander book

Published by Salamander Books Limited
LONDON • NEW YORK

Published 1989 by Salamander Books Ltd.,
52 Bedford Row, London WC1R 4LR

This book was created by Merehurst Limited
5 Great James Street, London WC1N 3DA

© 1989 Salamander Books Ltd.

ISBN: 0 86101 423 5

Commissioned and directed by Merehurst Limited
Managing Editor: Felicity Jackson
Editor: Louise Steele
Designer: Roger Daniels
Home Economist: Sarah Bush
Photographer: Jon Stewart, assisted by Kay Small
Typeset by Angel Graphics
Colour separation by Kentscan Limited
Printed in Belgium by Proost International Book Production

Companion volumes of interest:
The book of COCKTAILS
The book of CHOCOLATE & PETITS FOURS
The book of HORS D'OEUVRES
The book of GARNISHES
The book of PRESERVES
The book of SAUCES
The book of ICE CREAMS & SORBETS
The book of GIFTS FROM THE PANTRY
The book of HOT & SPICY NIBBLES – DIPS – DISHES
The book of PASTA
The book of BISCUITS
The book of CREPES & OMELETTES
The book of FONDUES
The book of CHEESECAKES
The book of SANDWICHES

CONTENTS

INTRODUCTION

Pizza can be found in practically every country of the world. They have, in the last 10-15 years, become one of the mainstays of convenience and fast food eating, with pizza restaurants almost everywhere. A wide selection of fresh and frozen pizzas are also widely available from food shops and supermarkets ready for cooking at home.

From humble beginnings – when it was sold in the streets of Naples – the pizza has risen to become a sophisticated way to eat a wealth of delicious ingredients from simple cheese and tomato, cooked with fresh herbs and olive oil, to exotic shellfish, oriental vegetables and spices.

It may be imagined that making pizza at home is a difficult task, but it isn't. True, the very best results are achieved by cooking them in the traditional brick built ovens. However, few of us will have that luxury at home and excellent results can be produced from your own oven, and with very little effort. Don't be put off by making a yeast dough – you will soon learn that it is just as easy as making pastry. You will also find that there are several delicious alternative pizza bases to choose from – wholemeal; scone-based; cornmeal and so on.

Pizza need not be just a snack or quick-cooked meal. They can become stylish cocktail foods, substantial pies and pasties – and even desserts – as you will see from the following pages. Included in the selection are ever-popular traditional recipes; deliciously quick and easy ideas, and pizzas designed especially for children. There is also a tempting range of pizzas to serve when entertaining, plus many international ideas – and an interesting selection of Italian breads.

One thing to remember. The pizza has an elegant history – being eaten by many a king or queen – so should never be considered simply a dumping ground for leftovers! It deserves better treatment than that and hopefully, with the help of *The Book of Pizzas and Italian Breads*, with over 100 easy-to-follow recipes, each illustrated with a splendid colour picture, you will discover a world of pizzas just waiting to be tasted!

THE HISTORY OF PIZZAS

In Naples one summer, around the late 1800's, Queen Margherita of Savoy was residing with her family in Capodimonte Park. She had heard a lot about pizza and decided to try it for herself. The local pizza maker was summoned and he served her a pizza with a newly invented topping. From then on, the tomato pulp, Mozzarella cheese and fresh basil pizza has been known as Pizza Margherita.

Until this time, pizza had been sold in the streets to people at breakfast, lunch and dinner. It was cut from a large tray that had been cooked in the baker's oven and had a simple topping made of mushrooms and anchovies.

As pizza became more popular, stalls were set up where the dough was shaped as customers ordered. Various toppings were invented including tomato, which had arrived from the New World. This soon developed into the opening of the Pizzeria, an open air place for folk to congregate, eat, drink and discuss. This has gradually become the pizza parlour we have today – which enjoys constant popularity – although the flavour of a pizza made, baked and eaten in the open air is unbeatable.

The dough base of the pizza has been baked in other countries of the Mediterranean for just as long. The French have their own Pissaladière recipe; for the Middle Eastern countries it's pitta bread and Spain uses the dough as a pastry for spicy savoury fillings. Even as far as China the same dough is steamed and served as individual stuffed snacks.

Although enjoying steady and constant popularity, it seems the pizza is now becoming a sophisticated, fashionable food with exotic toppings or turned into unusual shapes, large and small, with exciting fillings. Who knows what will happen to the pizza in years to come!

INGREDIENTS

The traditional pizzas of Italy rely on the wonderful Mediterranean ingredients that are so plentiful – sun-ripened tomatoes, thick olive oil, fresh herbs and cheese are the most well-known, but all sorts of other ingredients can be used as well. There may be some ingredients that you are not familar with.

Olive oil. Indispensable for making a genuine Italian pizza with the authentic flavour.
Olives. Both green and black are used. Olive pulp is made from crushed black olives and is obtainable in jars from Italian food shops and delicatessens.
Capers. These buds from a flowering plant have a delicious, though distinct flavour, so should be used with care.
Oregano(wild marjoram) is used on many pizzas. Use fresh wherever possible.
Thyme can be used fresh or dried.
Parsley, both flat and curly is used.

The small tender sprigs should be chosen and don't consider using the dried type for pizzas, the flavour is not nearly as good.
Basil is quite the best smelling of all the Italian herbs. Use the fresh type whenever possible.
Sweet marjoram is added to pizzas after they are cooked.
Sage should only be used fresh.
Mint should only be used fresh.
Black peppercorns should be used freshly ground as the aroma disappears very quickly, from the ready-ground type.
Nutmeg should be used freshly ground, to obtain the best flavour.
Chillies may be used in fresh form, or use whole dried or crushed type. Remember that chillies vary considerably in size and heat factor, so start with a small amount and gradually increase it.
Dried tomatoes in oil are a wonderful way to preserve tiny tomatoes. These have an unusual, distinct flavour and are available from Italian food shops and delicatessens.
Cheese. Mozzarella, Parmesan, Pecorino, Gorgonzola and Ricotta cheese are all used in traditional pizzas. (Parmesan and Pecorino are at their nicest when freshly grated from a solid piece.)

EQUIPMENT
Flat pizza tin. Metal is essential to conduct the heat and ensure that the base of the pizza is crisp.
Baking sheet. Can be used as an alternative to the flat pizza tin, however, a rim should be formed at the edge of the dough to keep the filling in place.
Rectangular tin or Swiss roll tin. For making the traditional Roman pizza or any that you wish to serve cut in squares.
Deep pan pizza tin. For the thick dough variety of pizza. A sandwich tin or pie tin may be used instead.
Pizza cutter. Makes the job of cutting a pizza far easier than using a knife.

— TRADITIONAL PIZZA DOUGH —

345 g (11 oz/2¾ cups) strong white flour
1 heaped teaspoon salt
15 g (½ oz/3 teaspoons) fresh (compressed) yeast; or 1 teaspoon dried active yeast and 1 teaspoon sugar; or 1 teaspoon easy blend yeast
185 ml (6 fl oz/¾ cup) hand-hot water
1 tablespoon olive oil

Put flour and salt in a large bowl.

In a small bowl, mix fresh yeast with a little water; put in a warm place until frothy. To use dried active yeast, whisk with sugar and a little water; leave until frothy. Add yeast liquid to flour with remaining water and oil. (To use easy blend yeast, mix into flour and salt before adding water and oil.) Mix to a soft dough; knead on floured surface for 10 minutes. Put in a greased bowl, cover; put in a warm place for 45 minutes or until doubled in size.

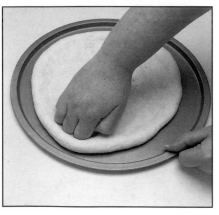

Knock back dough and knead briefly. Oil a 30 cm (12 in) pizza tin. Put dough in centre and press out to edges with knuckles. Pinch up edges to create a rim. Use as recipe instructs.

VARIATIONS

If preferred, the dough may be cooked in a 25 x 35.5 cm (10 in x 14 in) Swiss roll tin, or as 4 individual pizzas.

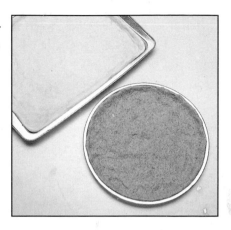

For Herb or Nut Pizza Dough: Knead 2 tablespoons chopped fresh herbs (or 1 tablespoon dried herbs) into the dough. If preferred, knead 30 g (1 oz/¼ cup) chopped walnuts into the dough.

For Wholemeal Pizza Dough: Use 315 g (10 oz/2¼ cups) wholemeal flour and 30 g (1 oz/¼ cup) wheat-germ. A little extra water may be required for mixing to form a soft dough. Follow the method given on page 10.

For Cornmeal Pizza Dough: Use 280 g (9 oz/2¼ cups) strong white flour and 60 g (2 oz/⅓ cup) corn-meal. Follow the method given on page 10.

POTATO PIZZA DOUGH

1 potato, about 155 g (5 oz) weight
345 g (11 oz/2¾ cups) strong white flour
1 heaped teaspoon salt
15 g (½ oz/3 teaspoons) fresh
(compressed) yeast; or 1 teaspoon dried
active yeast and 1 teaspoon sugar; or 1
teaspoon easy blend yeast
about 185 ml (6 fl oz/¾ cup) hand-hot
water

Scrub the unpeeled potato.

Boil in the skin for 30-40 minutes.
Drain and allow to cool sufficiently
to remove the skin.

Put flour and salt in a bowl. In a
small bowl, cream fresh yeast with a
little of the water and put in a warm
place until frothy. If using dried
active yeast, whisk together with
sugar and a little water and set
aside. If using easy blend yeast, mix
into flour and salt at this stage (do
not add any liquid).

Sieve potato directly into flour and stir in yeast with remaining water. If using easy blend yeast, add all the hand-hot water at this stage.

Mix to a soft dough, turn onto a lightly floured surface and knead for 10 minutes until smooth. Place in a clean, lightly oiled bowl and cover with plastic wrap. Put in a warm place for about 45 minutes until dough has doubled in size.

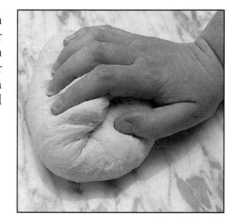

Knock back dough and knead briefly. Oil a 30 cm (12 in) pizza tin. Place dough in the centre and press out to edges with the knuckles. Pinch up edges to create a rim. Use as recipe instructs.

Variation: Knead 2 tablespoons chopped fresh herbs or 2 tablespoons freshly grated Parmesan cheese into the dough.

—— DEEP PAN PIZZA DOUGH ——

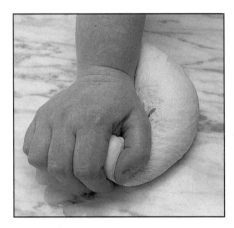

| 155 g (5 oz/1¼ cups) strong white flour |
| 155 g (5 oz/1¼ cups) plain flour |
| 1 heaped teaspoon salt |
| 15 g (½ oz/3 teaspoons) fresh (compressed) yeast; or 1 teaspoon dried active yeast and 1 teaspoon sugar; or 1 teaspoon easy blend yeast |
| 185 ml (6 fl oz/¾ cup) hand-hot water |
| 1 tablespoon olive oil |

Make dough as for Traditional Pizza Dough. When dough has doubled in size, knock back and knead briefly.

Thoroughly oil a 25 cm (10 in) deep pan pizza tin or sandwich tin. Place dough in the centre and press out to edges with the knuckles.

Cover with plastic wrap and put in a warm place for about 1½ hours, until risen almost to the top of tin. Use as recipe instructs.

CRUMBLE PIZZA DOUGH

185 g (6 oz/1½ cups) plain flour
1 teaspoon salt
2 teaspoons caster sugar
60 ml (2 fl oz/¼ cup) vegetable oil
6 teaspoons milk

Sift flour into a large bowl. Stir in salt and sugar. Whisk oil and milk together in measuring jug and pour onto the flour.

Stir with a fork until mixture is crumbly but still moist. It will not form the usual dense dough.

Press mixture onto base and up sides of a 25 cm (10 in) deep pan pizza tin or pie tin. Use as recipe instructs.

SCONE PIZZA DOUGH

125 g (4 oz/1 cup) self-raising wholewheat flour
125 g (4 oz/1 cup) self-raising white flour
salt and pepper
60 g (2 oz/¼ cup) butter or margarine
about 155 ml (5 fl oz/⅔ cup) milk

Put flours into a large bowl. Season. Add butter or margarine and rub in with the fingertips until mixture resembles breadcrumbs.

Stir in sufficient milk to form a dough. Turn onto a lightly floured surface and knead briefly.

Roll out dough to a circle measuring 25 cm (10 in). Transfer to a greased baking sheet and use as recipe instructs.

Variation: Stir 2 tablespoons chopped fresh parsley into crumb mixture before adding liquid.

PIZZA CARCIOFI

1 quantity Traditional Pizza Dough, shaped and ready for topping, see pages 10 and 11

TOPPING:

2 tablespoons Tomato Topping, see page 19

60 g (2 oz/½ cup) grated Fontina cheese

280 g (9 oz) jar artichokes in oil

8 preserved tomatoes in oil

salt and pepper

parsley, to garnish

Preheat oven to 220C (425F/Gas 7). Spread the dough with Tomato Topping. Sprinkle over the grated Fontina cheese.

Drain artichokes, reserving the oil. Drain the tomatoes. Slice artichokes and arrange over the cheese. Chop tomatoes roughly and sprinkle over the artichokes. Season to taste with salt and pepper. Sprinkle with 1-2 tablespoons of the reserved artichoke oil.

Bake in the oven for 20 minutes until dough is golden. Serve garnished with parsley.

Serves 4.

PIZZA NAPOLITANA

1 quantity Traditional Pizza Dough,
shaped and ready for topping, see pages 10
and 11

TOPPING:

3 tablespoons olive oil

500 g (1 lb) tomatoes

1 clove garlic, crushed

salt and pepper

250 g (8 oz) Mozzarella cheese

50 g (2 oz) can anchovy fillets, drained

1 tablespoon chopped fresh oregano

oregano sprigs, to garnish

Preheat oven to 220C (425F/Gas 7). Brush dough with 1 tablespoon oil. Place tomatoes in a bowl. Pour over boiling water. Leave for 1 minute. Drain, peel and roughly chop. Spread over dough. Sprinkle with garlic and season to taste with salt and pepper.

Slice cheese thinly. Arrange over tomatoes. Chop anchovies and sprinkle over cheese. Sprinkle over oregano and remaining oil. Bake in the oven for 20 minutes until cheese has melted and dough is crisp and golden. Serve the pizza at once, garnished with a few small sprigs of oregano.

Serves 4.

PIZZA MARGHERITA

1 quantity Traditional Pizza Dough, shaped and ready for topping, see pages 10 and 11

TOMATO TOPPING:

500 g (1 lb) tomatoes, skinned, see page 18, or 440 g (14 oz) can chopped tomatoes

2 tablespoons olive oil

1 onion, finely chopped

1 clove garlic, crushed

3 teaspoons tomato purée (paste)

½ teaspoon sugar

3 teaspoons chopped fresh basil

salt and pepper

TO FINISH:

1-2 tablespoons oil

125 g (4 oz) Mozzarella cheese

6-8 fresh basil leaves

basil sprig, to garnish

Make Tomato Topping. Chop tomatoes, if using fresh. Heat oil in saucepan. Add onion and garlic and cook until soft. Stir in tomatoes, tomato purée (paste), sugar and basil and season to taste with salt and pepper. Cover pan and simmer gently for 30 minutes until thick.

Preheat oven to 220C (425F/Gas 7). Brush dough with 1 tablespoon oil. Spoon over tomato topping. Slice Mozzarella thinly. Arrange over sauce. Sprinkle with salt to taste, 2-3 basil leaves and remaining oil. Bake in the oven for 20 minutes until cheese has melted and dough is crisp and golden. Sprinkle with remaining basil leaves. Serve at once, garnished with a sprig of basil.

Serves 4.

PIZZA MARINARA

1 quantity Traditional Pizza Dough, shaped and ready for topping, see pages 10 and 11
TOPPING:
3 tablespoons olive oil
250 g (8 oz) tomatoes, skinned, see page 18
3 large cloves garlic, peeled
salt and pepper
few capers, if desired

Preheat oven to 220C (425F/Gas 7). Brush dough with 1 tablespoon oil. Quarter tomatoes and discard seeds. Chop roughly and drain in a sieve. Spread over dough. Cut garlic into thick slices and sprinkle over tomatoes.

Season. Sprinkle with oil. Bake in the oven for 20 minutes until dough is crisp and golden. Sprinkle with capers, if desired.

Serves 4.

ROMAN PIZZA

1 quantity Traditional Pizza Dough, made up to end of step 2, see pages 10 and 11

TOPPING:

3 tablespoons olive oil

2 large onions, chopped

500 g (1 lb) tomatoes, skinned, see page 18, or 440 g (14 oz) can chopped tomatoes

185 g (6 oz) can red pimento, drained

50 g (2 oz) can anchovy fillets

12 stoned black olives

pimento and olives, to garnish

Preheat oven to 220C (425F/Gas 7). Lightly grease a 25 x 35.5 cm (10 x 14 in) Swiss roll tin. Knock back risen dough and knead briefly. Place in prepared tin and press out to edges with knuckles. Pinch up edges to create a rim.

In a saucepan, heat 2 tablespoons oil. Cook onions until soft. Chop tomatoes, if fresh, add to pan and cook for 2 minutes. Spoon over dough. Slice pimento in strips and arrange over tomato. Drain anchovies, cut in half lengthwise and arrange in a lattice pattern on top. Halve olives and place in gaps. Sprinkle with remaining oil.

Bake in the oven for 20 minutes until dough is crisp and golden. Garnish with pimento and olives.

Serves 4.

FOUR SEASONS PIZZA

1 quantity Traditional Pizza Dough, made up to end of step 2, see pages 10 and 11
TOPPING:
3 tablespoons olive oil
60 g (2 oz) button mushrooms
60 g (2 oz) prosciutto (Parma ham)
6 stoned black olives
4 canned artichoke hearts, drained
60 g (2 oz) Mozzarella cheese
1 tomato, skinned, see page 18
salt and pepper

Preheat oven to 220C (425F/Gas 7). Lightly grease a baking sheet. Knock back risen dough and knead briefly. Place dough on baking sheet, press out with knuckles to a circle measuring 25 cm (10 in). Brush dough with a little oil.

Heat 2 tablespoons oil in a saucepan. Cook mushrooms for 5 minutes. Mark dough into 4 equal sections with a knife. Arrange mushrooms over one section. Cut ham in strips and chop olives; place over second section. Slice artichokes thinly. Arrange over third section. Slice cheese and tomato and arrange over fourth section. Season to taste with salt and pepper. Sprinkle with remaining oil. Bake in the oven for 20 minutes until dough is crisp and golden. Serve at once.

Serves 4.

Variation: Make this recipe as 4 individual pizzas, if preferred.

— SPICY PORK & PEPPER PIZZA —

1 quantity Traditional Pizza Dough, shaped and ready for topping, see pages 10 and 11

TOPPING:

2 tablespoons olive oil

1 quantity Tomato Topping, see page 19

125 g (4 oz/1 cup) grated Mozzarella cheese

3-4 Italian pork sausages

salt and pepper

1 yellow pepper (capsicum), seeded and chopped

2 tablespoons freshly grated Parmesan cheese

chopped fresh parsley, to garnish

Preheat oven to 220C (425F/Gas 7). Brush dough with 1 tablespoon oil. Spread Tomato Topping over dough. Sprinkle Mozzarella on top. With a sharp knife, cut skins from sausages and discard. Break meat into pieces, scatter over cheese. Season to taste with salt and pepper.

Sprinkle with chopped pepper (capsicum), Parmesan cheese and remaining olive oil. Bake in the oven for 20 minutes until dough is crisp. Garnish with parsley.

Serves 4.

─ PROSCIUTTO & OLIVE PIZZA ─

1 quantity Traditional Pizza Dough,
shaped and ready for topping, see pages 10
and 11

TOPPING:

185 g (6 oz) Mozzarella cheese

4 slices prosciutto (Parma ham)

2 tablespoons olive pulp, see Note

2 tablespoons olive oil

salt and pepper

TO GARNISH:

prosciutto (Parma ham)

few olives

basil sprigs

Preheat oven to 220C (425F/Gas 7). Make the topping. Cut cheese and prosciutto (Parma ham) into cubes. Place in bowl with olive pulp. Mix together and moisten with a little oil if dry. Spread over dough. Season to taste with salt and pepper and sprinkle with remaining oil. Bake in the oven for 20 minutes until dough is crisp and golden. Garnish with curls of prosciutto (Parma ham), olives and basil sprigs.

Serves 4.

Note: Olive pulp may be bought in jars from Italian food shops.

ITALIAN SAUSAGE PIZZA

1 quantity Traditional Pizza Dough, shaped and ready for topping, see pages 10 and 11

TOPPING:

2 tablespoons olive oil

1 quantity Tomato Topping, see page 19

60 g (2 oz) mushrooms, finely sliced

3 spicy Italian sausages or 1 Luganeghe

2 tablespoons freshly grated Pecorino cheese

salt and pepper

extra grated Pecorino cheese and flat-leaf parsley, to garnish

Preheat oven to 220C (425F/Gas 7). Brush dough with 1 tablespoon oil. Spread Tomato Topping over dough and sprinkle with mushrooms. With a sharp knife, cut skins from the sausages and discard. Break meat into pieces and scatter over mushrooms. Sprinkle with grated cheese. Season to taste with salt and pepper.

Sprinkle remaining olive oil over top. Bake in the oven for 20 minutes until dough is crisp and golden. Serve garnished with extra grated Pecorino cheese and flat-leaf parsley.

Serves 4.

THREE PEPPER PIZZA

1 quantity Traditional Pizza Dough, shaped and ready for topping, see pages 10 and 11

TOPPING:

1 red pepper (capsicum)

1 yellow pepper (capsicum)

1 green pepper (capsicum)

2 tomatoes, skinned, see page 18

3 tablespoons olive oil

1 onion, finely chopped

1 clove garlic, crushed

salt and pepper

pinch of dried oregano

oregano sprigs and olives, to garnish

Make the topping. Skin peppers (capsicums): spear one at a time with a fork and hold over a gas flame for 5-10 minutes until black and blistered. Alternatively, halve and seed peppers (capsicums). Place under preheated grill until black. Peel skin off with a knife.

Chop red pepper (capsicum); quarter, seed and chop tomatoes. Put in a saucepan with 2 tablespoons oil, onion and garlic. Cook until soft. Preheat oven to 220C (425F/Gas 7). Brush dough with a little oil.

Spread pepper (capsicum) mixture over dough. Season to taste with salt and pepper. Sprinkle with oregano. Cut remaining peppers (capsicums) in strips. Arrange over pizza. Season to taste with salt and pepper. Sprinkle with remaining oil. Bake in the oven for 20 minutes until dough is crisp and golden. Garnish with oregano and olives.

Serves 4.

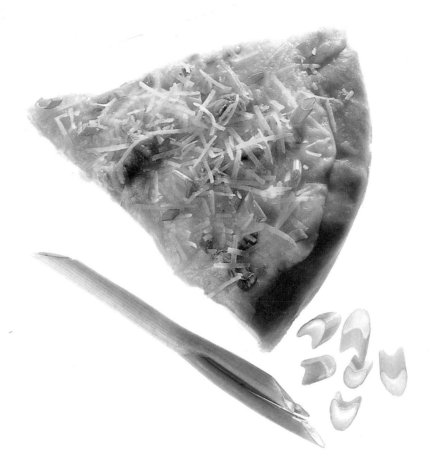

FOUR CHEESE PIZZA

1 quantity Traditional Pizza Dough,
shaped and ready for topping, see pages 10
and 11

TOPPING:

2 tablespoons olive oil

60 g (2 oz) Mozzarella cheese

60 g (2 oz) Gorgonzola cheese

60 g (2 oz) Fontina or Gruyère cheese

60 g (2 oz/½ cup) freshly grated Parmesan
cheese

salt and pepper

chopped spring onion and extra grated
cheese, to garnish

Preheat oven to 220C (425F/Gas 7). Brush dough with 1 tablespoon oil. Cut the 3 cheeses into small cubes. Sprinkle over the dough. Sprinkle over Parmesan, season to taste with salt and pepper. Sprinkle over remaining oil.

Bake in the oven for 20 minutes until cheese is melted and dough is crisp and golden. Garnish with spring onion and extra cheese.

Serves 4.

CRUMPET PIZZAS

4 rashers streaky bacon, rinds removed
8 crumpets
60 g (2 oz/¼ cup) butter
2 tablespoons anchovy paste
4 tomatoes, sliced
8 slices processed Cheddar cheese
4 spring onions
stuffed olives, to garnish

Preheat grill. Grill bacon and crumpets.

Meanwhile, in a bowl, beat butter and anchovy paste together. Spread a little on each crumpet. Arrange tomato slices on top.

Cut cheese slices diagonally into 4 triangular shapes. Arrange on top of crumpets. Grill briefly to melt cheese. Slice spring onions and sprinkle on top. Cut bacon rashers in half crosswise. Roll up and spear on cocktail sticks with stuffed olives. Use to garnish crumpets and serve at once.

Serves 4.

DEVILLED MUFFINS

4 wholemeal muffins

TOPPING:

2 tablespoons vegetable oil

1 tablespoon grated fresh root ginger, if desired

375 g (12 oz) mushrooms, sliced

1 bunch spring onions, sliced

2 teaspoons Worcestershire sauce

½ teaspoon French mustard

salt and pepper

butter for spreading, if desired

spring onion tassels, to garnish

Preheat oven to 200 C (400F/Gas 6). Split muffins. Toast under pre-heated grill on both sides.

Meanwhile make topping. Heat oil in a large saucepan. Add ginger, if desired, and fry for 10-15 seconds, stirring.

Add mushrooms; cook stirring for 1 minute. Add spring onions and continue to cook for 10 seconds. Add Worcestershire sauce and mustard and season to taste with salt and pepper. Butter muffins, if desired. Spoon mushroom mixture on top of muffins and bake in the oven for 2-3 minutes. Serve at once, garnished with spring onion tassels.

Serves 4.

AUBERGINE & TOMATO PIZZA

1 quantity Traditional Pizza Dough,
shaped and ready for topping, see pages 10
and 11

AUBERGINE TOPPING:

500 g (1 lb) aubergines (eggplants)

1 clove garlic, crushed

3 tablespoons lemon juice

3 tablespoons chopped fresh parsley

2 spring onions, chopped

salt and pepper

TO FINISH:

500 g (1 lb) tomatoes, sliced

1 tablespoon olive oil

2 tablespoons chopped fresh parsley

2 tablespoons freshly grated Parmesan
cheese

parsley sprigs, to garnish

First make Aubergine Topping.
Preheat oven to 180C (350F/Gas
4). Put aubergines (eggplants) on a
baking sheet and bake in the oven
for 30 minutes until soft. Cool.

Halve and scoop out soft centres
into a bowl. Add garlic, lemon
juice, parsley and spring onions.
Season to taste with salt and
pepper.

Increase oven temperature to
220C (425F/Gas 7). Spread aubergine (eggplant) purée over dough.
Arrange sliced tomatoes on top,
brush with oil and season to taste
with salt and pepper. Sprinkle with
chopped parsley and Parmesan
cheese. Bake in the oven for 20
minutes. Serve garnished with
parsley.

Serves 4.

Note: The aubergine purée may be
made in advance and refrigerated
for 3-4 days. It is also delicious
served as a dip with hot toast or
pitta bread.

NUTTY VEGETABLE PIZZA

1 quantity Scone Pizza Dough, shaped and ready for topping, see page 16

60 g (2 oz/⅓ cup) roasted peanuts, chopped

TOPPING:

¼ small white cabbage

2 carrots

2 sticks celery

2 tablespoons French dressing

salt and pepper

125 g (4 oz) full fat soft cheese, cubed

peanuts and celery leaves, to garnish

Preheat oven to 220C (425F/Gas 7). Cover dough with the chopped peanuts and press in lightly. Bake in the oven for 15 minutes.

Meanwhile, shred cabbage, grate carrots and slice celery thinly. Place vegetables in a bowl. Add the French dressing and season to taste with salt and pepper.

Spoon vegetables over the pizza. Arrange cubes of cheese on top. Return to oven and bake for a further 10 minutes. Serve at once, sprinkled with peanuts and garnished with celery leaves.

Serves 4.

─ PESTO & MUSHROOM PIZZA ─

1 quantity Deep Pan Pizza Dough, shaped and ready for topping, see page 14
PESTO TOPPING:
1 large bunch fresh basil leaves
3 cloves garlic, peeled
60 g (2 oz/⅓ cup) pine nuts
3 tablespoons freshly grated Parmesan cheese
salt and pepper
155 ml (5 fl oz/⅔ cup) olive oil
a little boiling water
TO FINISH:
185 g (6 oz) button mushrooms, sliced
a little olive oil
90 g (3 oz/⅔ cup) grated Mozzarella cheese
90 g (3 oz/⅔ cup) freshly grated Parmesan cheese
basil sprigs and pine nuts, to garnish

Preheat oven to 220C (425F/Gas 7). Make topping. In a blender or food processor, put basil leaves, garlic, pine nuts and Parmesan cheese and season to taste with salt and pepper. Switch on machine and pour in oil in a gentle stream until absorbed. Blend until smooth, adding a little boiling water if necessary, to achieve a spreading consistency.

Spread topping over dough. Arrange mushrooms on top; brush with olive oil. Sprinkle with Mozzarella cheese and Parmesan cheese. Bake in the oven for 20 minutes until dough is well risen and golden. Serve garnished with basil and pine nuts.

Serves 4.

Note: Pesto can be made in advance and stored in a screw-topped jar in the refrigerator for up to 6 days. Ready-made pesto may be bought from delicatessen counters in supermarkets and from specialist food shops.

— TAPENADE & PEPPER PIZZA —

1 quantity Deep Pan Pizza Dough, shaped and ready for topping, see page 14
TAPENADE TOPPING:
155 g (5 oz) stoned green olives
60 g (2 oz) can anchovy fillets
60 g (2 oz) canned tuna fish in oil, drained
30 g (1 oz) capers
1 clove garlic
1 teaspoon Dijon mustard
a little olive oil
salt and pepper
a little lemon juice
TO FINISH:
1 green pepper (capsicum), skinned, see page 26
1 yellow pepper (capsicum), skinned
mint sprigs and a few capers, to garnish

Preheat oven to 220C (425F/Gas 7). Make the topping. In a blender or food processor, put the olives, anchovy fillets and oil, tuna fish, capers, garlic and mustard. Blend to a rough-textured purée. Add a little extra oil if necessary. Season with salt and pepper and lemon juice.

Cut skinned peppers (capsicums) into strips and then into diamond shapes. Spread tapenade over dough. Arrange peppers attractively on top. Trickle a little more oil over and season with pepper. Bake in the oven for 20 minutes until dough is golden and well risen. Serve garnished with mint sprigs and capers.

Serves 4.

FRENCH BREAD PIZZA

1 medium French stick
4 tablespoons olive oil
440 g (14 oz) can tomatoes
salt and pepper
220 g (7 oz) can tuna fish in oil, drained
6-8 pimento-stuffed olives
60 g (2 oz/½ cup) grated Edam cheese
3 spring onions, chopped
TO SERVE:
green salad

Preheat oven to 180C (350F/Gas 4). Cut a slice from the top of French stick along whole length. Scoop out most of the soft crumb from base portion (this and the lid will not be required but can be used for breadcrumbs).

Brush inside of loaf with half the olive oil. Drain tomatoes and reserve juice. Brush inside of loaf with juice. Place loaf on a baking sheet and bake in the oven for 10 minutes.

Chop tomatoes and arrange half inside the loaf. Season to taste with salt and pepper. Flake tuna fish and spoon over tomatoes. Season again. Top with remaining tomatoes and season once again.

Halve olives and arrange on top. Sprinkle with grated cheese. Return to oven and bake for a further 15 minutes. Sprinkle with chopped spring onions and serve at once with salad.

Serves 2.

CHEESE & ONION PIZZAS

8 small pitta breads
CHEESE TOPPING:
30 g (1 oz/6 teaspoons) butter or margarine
15 g (½ oz/6 teaspoons) plain flour
250 g (8 oz/2 cups) grated Cheddar cheese
75 ml (2½ fl oz/⅓ cup) milk
1 egg yolk
pinch of dry mustard
pinch of cayenne pepper
TO FINISH:
3 spring onions, chopped
2 eggs, hard-boiled and chopped
hard-boiled egg and chives, to garnish

Preheat oven to 220C (425F/Gas 7). Make the topping. In a saucepan, melt butter or magarine. Add flour and cook, stirring, until smooth. Stir in half the grated cheese, then half the milk. Repeat with remaining cheese and milk. Beat in egg yolk. Stir in mustard and cayenne pepper and mix well.

Place pitta breads on a greased baking sheet. Spread topping over them. Bake in the oven for 10 minutes. In a bowl, mix chopped spring onions and hard-boiled eggs together. Sprinkle the mixture over the pizzas and cook for a further 2 minutes. Serve at once, garnished with slices of hard-boiled egg and chives.

Serves 4.

CREAMY SALMON PIZZA

1 quantity Wholemeal Pizza Dough, shaped and ready for topping, see pages 10 and 11

1 tablespoon olive oil

TOPPING:

439 g (15½ oz) can red salmon

1 courgette (zucchini), finely chopped

3 tablespoons double (thick) cream

salt and pepper

1 teaspoon grated lemon peel

1 tablespoon chopped fresh dill

30 g (1 oz/¼ cup) grated Parmesan cheese

lemon peel and dill sprigs, to garnish

Preheat oven to 220C (425F/Gas 7). Make the topping. Drain salmon and remove bones. Put in a bowl and flake with a fork. Stir in courgette (zucchini), cream, salt and pepper, lemon peel and dill.

Brush dough with olive oil. Spoon the salmon mixture on top. Sprinkle with the Parmesan cheese. Bake in the oven for 20 minutes until the dough is golden. Serve garnished with lemon and dill.

Serves 4.

CHEESY SEAFOOD PIZZA

1 quantity Traditional Pizza Dough,
shaped and ready for topping, see pages 10
and 11

TOPPING:

1 quantity Cheese Topping, see page 35

220 g (7 oz) can tuna fish in brine

185 g (6 oz) peeled prawns, thawed if
frozen

¼ teaspoon paprika

salt and pepper

lemon twists, coriander sprigs and peeled
prawns, to garnish, if desired

Preheat oven to 220C (425F/Gas
7). Spread the Cheese Topping
over the pizza dough.

Drain tuna fish, put in a bowl and
flake roughly with a fork. Mix in
prawns and paprika and season to
taste with salt and pepper. Spread
mixture evenly over the Cheese
Topping.

Bake in the oven for 20 minutes
until the dough is crisp and
golden. Serve the pizza at once,
garnished with lemon twists, sprigs
of coriander and peeled prawns, if
desired.

Serves 4.

FRITTATA PIZZA

1 quantity Traditional Pizza Dough, made
up to end of step 2, see pages 10 and 11

TOPPING:

2 tablespoons olive oil

1 onion, thinly sliced

3 new potatoes, cooked and sliced

8 slices pepper salami, rind removed

1 small green pepper (capsicum), sliced

8 stoned black olives, halved

60 g (2 oz/⅓ cup) full fat soft cheese,
cubed

1 tablespoon chopped fresh parsley

4 cherry tomatoes, halved

6 eggs

salt and pepper

watercress, to garnish

Preheat oven to 220C (425F/Gas
7). Grease a 25 cm (10 in) deep pan
pizza tin or sandwich tin. Knock
back risen dough and knead briefly,
then press dough into tin.

Brush dough with a little of the
oil. Arrange sliced onion over the
top. Sprinkle with remaining oil.
Bake in the oven for 10 minutes.

Remove pizza from oven. Arrange sliced potatoes, salami, pepper (capsicum), olives and cheese
over the surface. Add parsley and
tomatoes. In a bowl, beat together
eggs and season to taste with salt
and pepper. Pour over pizza and bake
for 10-15 minutes until topping is
puffed and golden. Serve garnished
with watercress.

Serves 4.

TOMATO & MINT PIZZA

1 quantity Scone Pizza Dough, shaped and ready for topping, see page 16

TOPPING:

1 tablespoon vegetable oil

250 g (8 oz) cherry tomatoes

salt and pepper

1 large onion, sliced thinly

90 g (3 oz/⅔ cup) grated Red Leicester or red cheese

2 tablespoons chopped fresh mint

natural yogurt, to serve

mint sprigs, to garnish

Preheat oven to 220C (425F/Gas 7). Brush dough with oil. Halve tomatoes and arrange over dough. Season to taste with salt and pepper. Arrange onion slices on top. Sprinkle with grated cheese and chopped mint.

Bake in the oven for 20 minutes until dough is golden brown and cheese is bubbling. Serve at once, with natural yogurt, garnished with sprigs of mint.

Serves 4.

Variation: Ordinary Cheddar cheese can be used instead of red cheese.

GRAVLAX MUFFINS

6 muffins
TOPPING:
125 g (4 oz/½ cup) butter, softened
1 teaspoon honey
2 teaspoons French mustard
2 teaspoons lemon juice
1 tablespoon chopped fresh dill
salt and pepper
350 g (12 oz) gravlax or smoked salmon
thick sour cream and dill sprigs,
to garnish

Preheat oven to 220C (425F/Gas 7). Halve the muffins and place them on a baking sheet. Bake in the oven for 5 minutes.

Meanwhile, in a bowl beat the butter with the honey, French mustard, lemon juice and chopped fresh dill. Season to taste with salt and pepper.

Spread the butter mixture over the muffins and top with the gravlax or smoked salmon, dividing it equally between them. Bake in the oven for 5 minutes, then serve at once, garnished with thick sour cream and sprigs of dill.

Serves 6.

AVOCADO & CRAB BITES

1 quantity Traditional Pizza Dough, made up to end of step 2, see pages 10 and 11

TOPPING:

2 ripe avocados

1 tablespoon lemon juice

30 g (1 oz/6 teaspoons) butter

30 g (1 oz/¼ cup) plain flour

315 ml (10 fl oz/1¼ cups) milk

salt and pepper

¼ teaspoon cayenne pepper

375 g (12 oz) crabmeat, thawed if frozen and drained

60 g (2 oz/½ cup) grated Gruyère cheese

avocado slices and tomato, to garnish

Preheat oven to 220C (425F/Gas 7). Knock back risen dough and knead briefly. Roll out dough and use to line a Swiss roll tin.

Make topping. Halve avocados, remove stones. Scoop out flesh and chop roughly. Place in a bowl with lemon juice and stir lightly to coat. Set aside.

Melt butter in a saucepan. Stir in flour and cook for 2 minutes. Stir in milk, bring to the boil and simmer for 2 minutes. Season to taste with salt and pepper and cayenne.

Remove pan from heat. Stir in crab, cheese and avocado. Spread over the dough, then bake in the oven for 20 minutes until dough is golden. Cool slightly before cutting into fingers or squares. Serve garnished with avocado and tomato.

Serves 6-8.

— CORONATION CHICKEN PIZZA —

1 quantity Traditional Pizza Dough, shaped and ready for topping, see pages 10 and 11

TOPPING:

375 g (12 oz) cooked chicken meat, cubed

60 g (2 oz/⅓ cup) roasted cashew nuts

1 small leek, finely shredded

3 tablespoons mayonnaise

3 tablespoons Greek natural yogurt

1 teaspoon curry powder

1 tablespoon apricot jam

1 tablespoon mango chutney, chopped

2 tablespoons chopped fresh coriander

salt and pepper

lemon juice, to taste

coriander, to garnish

Preheat oven to 220C (425F/Gas 7). Make the topping. In a bowl, mix chicken, cashew nuts and leek. In a second bowl, mix mayonnaise, yogurt, curry powder, jam, chutney and coriander. Season to taste with salt and pepper and lemon juice. Mix sauce with the chicken mixture. Spoon chicken mixture on top of the dough. Bake in the oven for 20 minutes until the dough is golden. Serve at once, garnished with coriander.

Serves 4.

Variation: Substitute other cooked and cubed meat, such as ham, pork, or lamb for the chicken and use roasted almonds, roughly chopped, instead of the cashew nuts.

— TARRAGON TROUT PARCEL —

1 quantity Potato Pizza Dough, made up to end of step 5, see pages 12 and 13

FILLING:

500 g (1 lb) pink trout fillets, skinned

625 ml (20 fl oz/2½ cups) white wine

few parsley and tarragon sprigs

salt and pepper

60 g (2 oz/¼ cup) butter

60 g (2 oz/½ cup) plain flour

2 tablespoons single (light) cream

125 g (4 oz) peeled prawns, thawed if frozen

60 g (2 oz) mushrooms, sliced

beaten egg, to glaze

4 teaspoons sesame seeds

prawns, lemon and tarragon sprigs, to garnish

Make the filling. Put fish and wine in a saucepan with parsley and tarragon sprigs and season with a little salt and pepper. Bring to the boil, cover and remove from the heat. Leave to cool. Drain and reserve liquor. Flake fish.

Melt butter in a saucepan. Add flour and cook, stirring. Add reserved liquid to make a smooth sauce. Remove from heat, stir in fish, cream, prawns and mushrooms. Check seasoning. Cool.

Preheat oven to 220C (425F/Gas 7). Grease a baking sheet. Knock back risen dough and knead briefly. Roll out dough on a lightly floured surface to a square measuring 30 cm (12 in). Place on baking sheet. Spoon filling in centre. Brush edges with beaten egg. Fold corners of dough to centre; pinch seams to seal. Brush with beaten egg and sprinkle with sesame seeds. Bake for 25-30 minutes. Serve garnished with prawns, lemon and tarragon.

Serves 4-6.

HAM & TOMATO BITES

1 quantity Traditional Pizza Dough, made
to end of step 2, see pages 10 and 11

TOPPING:

1 quantity Tomato Topping, see page 19
12-14 slices coppa, or Parma, smoked ham
185 g (6 oz) Mozzarella cheese, sliced
olives, anchovies and thyme sprigs, to
garnish

Preheat oven to 220C (425F/Gas
7). Grease several baking sheets.
Roll out dough very thinly and cut
out 12-14 circles with a 4-5 cm
(1½-2 in) cutter.

Spread dough with Tomato Topping. Top each circle with a slice of
coppa, or Parma, ham and a slice of
Mozzarella. Bake in the oven for
10-15 minutes until the dough is
cooked and the cheese has melted.
Serve at once, garnished with
olives, anchovies and thyme.

Serves 6-8.

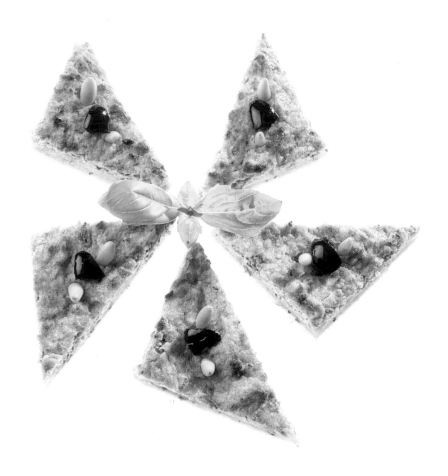

PESTO PIZZELLE

1 quantity Traditional Pizza Dough, made to end of step 2, see pages 10 and 11

TOPPING:

185 g (6 oz) ricotta cheese

3 tablespoons Pesto Topping, see page 32

1 egg, beaten

basil sprigs, black olives and pine nuts, to garnish

Preheat oven to 220C (425F/Gas 7). Knock back risen dough and knead briefly. Roll out dough and use to line a Swiss roll tin.

Make the topping. Beat together ricotta cheese and sufficient Pesto Topping and egg to make a smooth, firm mixture.

Spread over the dough, then bake in the oven for 20 minutes until the dough is golden. Cool slightly, then cut into squares or triangles. Garnish with basil, olives and pine nuts. Serve as a cocktail snack.

Serves 10-20.

FRESH HERB PIZZA

1 quantity Scone Pizza Dough, shaped and ready for topping, see page 16

TOPPING:

2 tablespoons olive oil
1 tablespoon chopped fresh basil
1 tablespoon chopped fresh parsley
1 teaspoon chopped fresh oregano
185 g (6 oz/1 ½ cups) grated Mozzarella cheese
90 g (3 oz/¾ cup) grated Pecorino cheese
salt and pepper
fresh herbs, to garnish

Preheat oven to 220C (425F/Gas 7). Brush the dough with 1 tablespoon oil. Sprinkle with chopped herbs. Cover with the cheeses and season to taste with salt and pepper. Drizzle over the remaining oil. Bake in the oven to 20 minutes until golden. Serve garnished with herbs.

Serves 4.

ASPARAGUS HAM SQUARES

1 quantity Traditional Pizza Dough, made up to end of step 2, see pages 10 and 11

1 tablespoon vegetable oil

TOPPING:

185 g (6 oz) sliced ham

185 g (6 oz) curd cheese

2 tablespoons single (light) cream or milk

250 g (8 oz) asparagus spears, cooked

salt and pepper

freshly grated Parmesan cheese

Preheat oven to 220 C (425F/Gas 7). Grease a 25 x 35.5 cm (10 x 14 in) Swiss roll tin. Knock back risen dough and knead briefly. Roll out dough on a lightly floured surface and use to line base and sides of tin. Prick base with a fork. Brush with oil. Bake in the oven for 15 minutes until crisp and golden.

Meanwhile, finely chop 125 g (4 oz) ham. Put in a bowl with the cheese and cream or milk. Cut tips from asparagus and reserve. Chop stalks and stir into cheese mixture.

Remove pizza from oven and allow to cool slightly. Spread cheese mixture over dough. Slice remaining ham in strips and arrange in a lattice pattern over dough. Dot asparagus tips on surface, season to taste with salt and pepper and sprinkle with Parmesan cheese. Return to oven and cook for a further 2 minutes. Slide pizza from tin onto a chopping board. With a sharp knife cut off crusts and discard. Cut pizza into small squares or fingers (or other shapes, if preferred) and serve as a cocktail snack.

Serves 8-10.

RATATOUILLE & PRAWN PIZZA

1 quantity Wholemeal Pizza Dough, shaped and ready for topping, see pages 10 and 11

1 tablespoon vegetable oil

TOPPING:

2 tablespoons vegetable oil

1 large onion, chopped

2 cloves garlic, crushed

3 small courgettes (zucchini), halved

1 small red pepper (capsicum), seeded

1 small green pepper (capsicum), seeded

1 small yellow pepper (capsicum), seeded

250 g (8 oz) aubergine (eggplant), cubed

440 g (14 oz) can chopped tomatoes

2 tablespoons tomato purée (paste)

salt and pepper

125 g (4 oz) peeled prawns, thawed if frozen

chopped parsley, to garnish

Make the topping. Heat oil in a large saucepan. Add onion and garlic. Cook for 3 minutes, stirring and taking care not to let garlic burn.

Cut courgettes (zucchini) and peppers (capsicums) into 1 cm (½ in) pieces. Add to pan with aubergine (eggplant). Add tomatoes, tomato purée (paste) and season to taste with salt and pepper. Stir well and cook for 15 minutes until vegetables are cooked and the sauce thickened.

Preheat oven to 220 C (425F/Gas 7). Prick dough with a fork and brush with oil. Bake in the oven for 15 minutes. Stir prawns into vegetables and spoon on top of dough. Bake for a further 5 minutes. Serve at once sprinkled with chopped parsley.

Serves 4.

MIXED SEAFOOD PIZZA

1 quantity Traditional Pizza Dough, shaped and ready for topping, see pages 10 and 11

TOPPING:

250 g (8 oz) mussels in the shell

2 tablespoons olive oil

2 cloves garlic, crushed

125 g (4 oz) squid, cleaned

440 g (14 oz) can chopped tomatoes

salt and pepper

125 g (4 oz) raw Mediterranean (king) prawns, thawed if frozen

250 g (8 oz) clean shelled clams or 144 g (14 oz) canned clams in brine, drained

2 tablespoons chopped fresh parsley

flat-leaf parsley and lemon, to garnish

Make topping. Scrub mussels and remove beards. Place in a large saucepan with 2 tablespoons water. Cover and cook over moderate heat, shaking pan, until all the shells are open.

Strain pan juices and reserve. In a saucepan, heat 1 tablespoon oil and garlic. Slice squid and add to pan. Cook for 5 minutes, stirring. Remove with a slotted spoon and reserve. Discard garlic. Add tomatoes, reserved mussel juice and season to taste with salt and pepper. Cook gently for 30 minutes.

Preheat oven to 220 C (425 F/Gas 7). Brush dough with remaining oil; prick with a fork. Bake in the oven for 15-20 minutes until golden. Peel prawns; add to sauce with the clams. Cook for 10 minutes. Stir in squid and mussels. Remove pizza from oven. Spoon over fish and sauce, sprinkle with chopped parsley and return to oven for 10 minutes. Garnish with parsley and lemon and serve at once.

Serves 4.

PIZZA CANAPÉS

1 quantity Cornmeal Pizza Dough, made up to end of step 2, see pages 10 and 11

TOPPING:

1 quantity Cheese Topping, see page 35
a selection of the following: anchovy fillets, stuffed and plain; olives; capers; lumpfish roe; cooked prawns; smoked salmon; crispy bacon; smoked quails' eggs; sprigs of fresh herbs

Preheat oven to 220C (425F/Gas 7). Grease several baking sheets. Knock back risen dough and knead briefly. Roll out dough very thinly and cut out 10-12 small circles with a 4-5 cm (1½-2 in) cutter (or cut into fingers, if preferred). Spread with a little Cheese Topping and arrange on baking sheets. Bake in the oven for 15-20 minutes until golden. Top with any selection of toppings and serve at once.

Serves 10-12.

HAM & CHEESE PARTY PIZZAS

1 quantity Cornmeal Pizza Dough, made up to end of step 2, see pages 10 and 11
1 tablespoon olive oil
TOPPING:
1 quantity Tomato Topping, see page 19
6 slices prosciutto (Parma ham)
10-12 stoned black or green olives
freshly grated Parmesan cheese and thyme sprigs, to garnish

Preheat oven to 220C (425F/Gas 7). Grease several baking sheets. Knock back risen dough and knead briefly. Roll out dough and cut as for Pizza Canapés, see page 50. Brush with oil and bake in the oven for 15-20 minutes until golden.

Spread each circle with a little Tomato Topping. Cut prosciutto into 10-12 pieces. Fold each piece into a cornet shape and place on top of a circle. Place an olive in each cone and sprinkle with Parmesan cheese. Return to oven for 3 minutes to soften cheese. Serve at once, garnished with cheese and thyme.

Serves 10-12.

GORGONZOLA & NUT SHAPES

1 quantity Traditional Pizza Dough, made
up to end of step 2, see pages 10 and 11

TOPPING:

185 g (6 oz) Gorgonzola cheese

185 g (6 oz) Mozzarella cheese

10 walnut halves

3 tablespoons walnut oil

cucumber, to garnish

Preheat oven to 220C (425F/Gas
7). Grease a 25 x 35.5 cm (10 x 14
in) Swiss roll tin. Knock back risen
dough and knead briefly. Roll out
dough on a lightly floured surface
and use to line base and sides of tin.
Cut Gorgonzola and Mozzarella

cheeses into small cubes. Roughly
chop walnuts. Brush surface of
dough with a little walnut oil.
Sprinkle cheese over and top with
walnuts. Sprinkle with remaining
oil.

Bake in the oven for 20 minutes
until dough is crisp and golden.
Slide from tin onto a chopping
board. Cut crusts off with a sharp
knife and discard. Cut pizza into
small squares and fingers. Garnish
with cucumber and serve at once as
a cocktail snack.

Serves 8-10.

MOZZOLIVE BITES

1 quantity Cornmeal Pizza Dough, made up to end of step 2, see pages 10 and 11
TOPPING:
4 tablespoons olive oil
185 g (6 oz) Mozzarella cheese
170 g (5½ oz) jar olive paste
salt and pepper
sage leaves and pimento, to garnish

Preheat oven to 220C (425F/Gas 7). Grease several baking sheets. Knock back risen dough and knead briefly. Roll out dough and cut as for Pizza Canapés, see page 50. Brush with 1 tablespoon oil and bake in the oven for 15-20 minutes until golden.

Cut Mozzarella into tiny pieces and place in a bowl. Stir in the olive paste. Season to taste with salt and pepper. Spoon a little of the mixture onto each circle, dividing it equally between them.

Sprinkle with a little oil. Bake for a further 3-4 minutes until cheese melts. Garnish with sage leaves and pimento. Serve at once as a cocktail snack.

Serves 10-12.

ARTICHOKE & EMMENTAL PIZZA

1 quantity Traditional Pizza Dough,
shaped and ready for topping, see pages 10
and 11

TOPPING:

3 tablespoons olive oil

440 g (14 oz) can artichoke hearts

salt and pepper

250 g (8 oz/2 cups) grated Emmental
cheese

marjoram leaves and sliced pimento, to
garnish

Preheat oven to 220C (425F/Gas 7). Brush the pizza dough with 1 tablespoon of the olive oil.

Drain artichokes and slice thinly. Arrange artichoke slices over dough. Sprinkle with remaining oil; season to taste with salt and pepper. Sprinkle the grated Emmental cheese over the top.

Bake in the oven for 20 minutes until dough is crisp and golden and cheese has melted. Serve at once, garnished with marjoram leaves and sliced pimento.

Serves 4.

—— THREE SALAMI PIZZA ——

1 quantity Scone Pizza Dough, shaped and ready for topping, see page 16
1 tablespoon vegetable oil
TOPPING:
3 tomatoes, finely chopped
salt and pepper
125 g (4 oz) mixed sliced salami, rinds removed
60 g (2 oz/½ cup) grated Cheddar cheese
gherkins, to garnish

Preheat oven to 220C (425F/Gas 7). Brush dough with the oil.

Spread tomatoes over surface. Season to taste with salt and pepper. Cut salami into strips and arrange over tomatoes. Sprinkle with grated cheese. Bake in the oven for 20 minutes until dough is golden and cheese melted. Serve garnished with gherkins.

Serves 4.

— MUSHROOM & CHEESE PIZZA —

1 quantity Wholemeal Pizza Dough,
shaped and ready for topping, see pages 10
and 11

TOPPING:

1-2 tablespoons French mustard or 30 g
(1 oz/6 teaspoons) butter or margarine,
melted

125 g (4 oz) sliced ham

125 g (4 oz) mushrooms, sliced

6 tablespoons crushed, sieved tomatoes

125 g (4 oz/1 cup) grated Cheddar cheese

salt and pepper

watercress sprigs, to garnish

Preheat oven to 220C (425F/Gas
7). Spread dough with the French
mustard, if using, or brush with the
melted butter or margarine.

Slice the ham diagonally to form
diamond shapes. Arrange over
dough. Place one-third of the
mushrooms in the centre and the
remainder in groups around the
edge of the pizza. Spoon a little
tomato over mushrooms. Sprinkle
with grated cheese. Season to taste
with salt and pepper and bake in the
oven for 20 minutes until dough is
crisp and golden and the cheese
bubbling. Garnish with watercress.

Serves 6.

SAUSAGE & ONION PIZZA

1 quantity Traditional Pizza Dough, shaped and ready for topping, see pages 10 and 11

TOPPING:

500 g (1 lb) pork chipolata sausages

30 g (1 oz/6 teaspoons) butter or margarine

1 large onion, finely sliced

125 g (4 oz) mushrooms, quartered

4 tablespoons sieved tomatoes

celery leaves, to garnish

Preheat oven to 220C (425F/Gas 7). Make topping. Heat grill on high. Cook sausages. Meanwhile, melt butter in a saucepan and cook onion gently until soft. Add mushrooms and tomatoes and cook, stirring, for 5 minutes. Drain sausages on absorbent kitchen paper. Slice diagonally.

Spoon the onion mixture over dough and top with sausage slices. Bake in the oven for 20 minutes until dough is crisp and golden. Serve garnished with celery leaves.

Serves 6.

SAUSAGE & APPLE PIZZA

1 quantity Wholemeal Pizza Dough,
made up to end of step 2, see pages 10
and 11

2 tablespoons vegetable oil

TOPPING:

500 g (1 lb) pork sausages with herbs

1 cooking apple, cored

3 tablespoons apple juice or cider

2 tablespoons mild mustard

salt and pepper

1 red eating apple

1 green eating apple

a little lemon juice

TO SERVE:

small packet potato crisps

Preheat oven to 200C (400F/Gas
6). Lightly grease a 25 x 35.5 cm
(10 x 14 in) Swiss roll tin. Knock
back risen dough and knead briefly.
Place in tin and press over base and

up sides with the knuckles. Brush
with 1 tablespoon oil.

Remove skin from the sausages
by splitting with a sharp knife. Put
sausagemeat in a bowl. Grate cooking apple, stir into sausagemeat with
apple juice or cider and mustard and
season to taste with salt and pepper.
Spread the mixture evenly over
pizza dough.

Core red and green eating apples.
Slice thinly and brush cut surfaces
with lemon juice. Arrange over
sausagemeat and brush with remaining 1 tablespoon oil. Bake in
the oven for 20 minutes until dough
is crisp and golden. Crush potato
crisps roughly and sprinkle over top
of pizza.

Serves 6.

POTATO PIZZA SQUARES

1 quantity Wholemeal Pizza Dough, made up to end of step 2, see pages 10 and 11

1 tablespoon vegetable oil

TOPPING:

8 small potatoes, peeled

salt

1 quantity Tomato Topping, see page 19

60 g (2 oz/½ cup) grated Cheddar cheese

cucumber slices and sliced spring onion, to garnish

Cook potatoes for topping in salted boiling water for 10-15 minutes. Drain, cool slightly; slice thinly.

Meanwhile, preheat oven to 220 C (425F/Gas 7). Grease a Swiss roll tin. Knock back risen dough and knead briefly. Roll out and use to line the Swiss roll tin. Brush with oil.

Spread Tomato Topping over dough. Arrange potato slices on top and sprinkle with grated cheese. Bake in the oven for 20 minutes. Serve cut into squares, garnished with cucumber and spring onion.

Serves 6-8.

PIZZA FACES

freshly-baked or bought, ready-made
individual pizza bases

TOPPING:

4 tablespoons tomato ketchup (sauce) or
chutney

6-8 processed Cheddar cheese slices

alfalfa sprouts or grated carrot

olive slices

pepper (capsicum) strips

Preheat oven to 200C (400F/Gas 6). Spread pizza bases with ketchup or chutney. Arrange cheese over top to represent skin. Place on a baking sheet and bake in the oven for 10-15 minutes until melted.

Give each child the prepared ingredients to make their own pizza face, using alfalfa sprouts or carrot as hair, olive slices for eyes and pepper (capsicum) strips for mouth.

Serves 2.

Variations: Many other ingredients can be used in place of those listed and children will enjoy making different expressions on the faces.

BLT PIZZA

1 quantity Traditional Pizza Dough, shaped and ready for topping, see pages 10 and 11

FILLING:

8 streaky bacon rashers, rinds removed

½ small iceberg lettuce

4 tomatoes, roughly chopped

4-6 tablespoons mayonnaise

salt and pepper

shredded lettuce, to garnish

Preheat oven to 200C (400F/Gas 6). Grill bacon until cooked. Drain on absorbent kitchen paper, then with kitchen scissors, cut into pieces. Very finely shred the lettuce. In a bowl, mix bacon, tomatoes, lettuce and mayonnaise and season to taste with salt and pepper.

Spread the mixture over the dough. Bake in the oven for 20 minutes until the dough is crisp and golden. Serve at once, garnished with shredded lettuce.

Serves 4.

GAMMON & PINEAPPLE PIZZA

8 crumpets

TOPPING:

1 quantity Cheese Topping, see page 35

185 g (6 oz) cooked gammon or shoulder ham, minced or finely chopped

salt and pepper

8 canned pineapple rings

chopped parsley, tomato wedges and pineapple, to garnish

Preheat oven to 220C (425F/Gas 7). Spread Cheese Topping evenly over crumpets. Pile ham on top. Season with salt and pepper.

Place a pineapple ring on each crumpet. Bake in the oven for 10-15 minutes. Serve garnished with parsley and a cocktail stick speared with pineapple and tomato.

Serves 8.

BREAKFAST PIZZA

1 quantity Traditional Pizza Dough, shaped and ready for topping, see pages 10 and 11

3 tablespoons vegetable oil

TOPPING:

440 g (14 oz) can chopped tomatoes

salt and pepper

8 streaky bacon rashers, rinds removed

4 eggs

Preheat oven to 220C (425F/Gas 7). Brush dough with 1 tablespoon oil.

Spoon chopped tomatoes over dough. Season to taste with salt and pepper. Arrange bacon over the tomatoes, leaving 4 gaps, equally spaced. Sprinkle with remaining oil and bake in the oven for 15 minutes.

Remove from oven. Break an egg into each of the 4 gaps. Return pizza to oven for about 10 minutes until the whites are set but the yolks still liquid. Serve at once.

Serves 4.

MINCE & PICKLE PIZZA

1 quantity Potato Pizza Dough, shaped and ready for topping, see pages 12 and 13

TOPPING:

250 g (8 oz) ground beef

salt and pepper

2 tablespoons tomato purée (paste)

2 tablespoons Worcestershire sauce

3 tablespoons vegetable oil

4 tablespoons sweet pickle

125 g (4 oz) mushrooms, sliced

1 green pepper (capsicum), sliced

1 small onion, sliced

watercress, chives and red pepper (capsicum), to garnish

Make the topping. In a saucepan, cook the beef until browned. Season to taste with salt and pepper. Add tomato purée (paste) and Worcestershire sauce. Cook for 15 minutes, stirring the mixture occasionally.

Preheat oven to 220C (425F/Gas 7). Brush dough with 1 tablespoon oil. Spread pickle over the dough. Arrange mushrooms on top. Spoon meat mixture on top. Arrange rings of pepper (capsicum) and onion over and brush with remaining oil. Bake in the oven for 20 minutes until dough is crisp and golden. Serve garnished with watercress bunches tied with chives and red pepper (capsicum).

Serves 4.

— SARDINE & TOMATO PIZZA —

1 quantity Traditional Pizza Dough, shaped and ready for topping, see pages 10 and 11
TOPPING:
4 tablespoons tomato ketchup (sauce)
125 g (4 oz) can sardines in oil, drained
2 tomatoes, sliced
4 processed cheese slices
mustard and cress, to garnish

Preheat oven to 220C (425F/Gas 7). Spread tomato ketchup (sauce) over the dough. Split sardines horizontally and arrange around the edge. Make a circle of overlapping tomatoes in the centre.

Cut cheese in strips and arrange in a lattice over the tomatoes. Bake in the oven for 20 minutes until the dough is golden. Serve at once, garnished with mustard and cress.

Serves 6.

BOLOGNESE PIZZA

1 quantity Potato Pizza Dough, with Parmesan cheese, shaped and ready for topping, see pages 12 and 13

TOPPING:

2 tablespoons vegetable oil

60 g (2 oz) rashers streaky bacon, chopped

1 onion, finely chopped

1 carrot, finely chopped

1 stick celery, finely chopped

1 clove garlic, crushed

250 g (8 oz) ground beef

1 tablespoon tomato purée (paste)

pinch of mixed herbs

125 ml (4 fl oz/½ cup) beef stock

salt and pepper

TO SERVE:

freshly grated Parmesan cheese

tomato and marjoram sprigs, to garnish

Make the topping. In a saucepan, heat oil and cook the bacon for 2 minutes. Add onion, carrot, celery and garlic. Cook, stirring, until soft. Add ground beef and cook, stirring until brown.

Stir in tomato purée (paste), herbs and stock and season to taste with salt and pepper. Cover and cook gently for 30 minutes.

Preheat oven to 220 C (425F/Gas 7). Spoon sauce on top of dough and spread over. Bake in the oven for 20 minutes until dough is crisp and golden. Serve sprinkled with Parmesan cheese and garnished with tomato and marjoram.

Serves 6.

TUNA & ONION PIZZA

1 quantity Deep Pan Pizza Dough, shaped
and ready for topping, see page 14

TOPPING:

2 tablespoons vegetable oil

440 g (14 oz) can chopped tomatoes

1 bunch spring onions, chopped

220 g (7 oz) can tuna fish, drained

salt and pepper

Preheat oven to 220C (425F/Gas
7). Brush dough with 1 tablespoon
oil. Bake in the oven for 20 minutes
until golden and well risen.

Make the topping. In a saucepan, heat the tomatoes and remaining oil. Add half the spring onions
to pan and cook for 10 minutes.
Flake tuna fish roughly, stir into
tomato mixture. Season to taste
with salt and pepper.

Spoon onto dough and bake in
the oven for 3-5 minutes. Shred
remaining chopped spring onions
and sprinkle over pizza to serve.

Serves 6.

STEAK & KIDNEY PIZZA

1 quantity Traditional Pizza Dough, shaped and ready for topping, see pages 10 and 11

TOPPING:

500 g (1 lb) sirloin steak, trimmed

250 g (8 oz) lambs' kidneys

2 tablespoons vegetable oil

1 onion, chopped

1 tablespoon plain flour

155 ml (5 fl oz/²⁄₃ cup) stock

155 ml (5 fl oz/²⁄₃ cup) red wine

salt and pepper

½ teaspoon dried thyme

thyme sprigs, to garnish

Cut meat in even-sized strips. Halve kidneys, remove cores and cut each half into 2 pieces. Heat oil in a large saucepan and cook onion for 5 minutes until golden. Remove with slotted spoon and reserve.

Brown the meat in oil, a little at a time. Using a slotted spoon, remove meat as soon as it is cooked and reserve. Add flour to pan and stir well, scraping up sediment. Stir in stock and wine. Season to taste with salt and pepper. Add thyme, bring to the boil, then reduce heat and cook until the mixture is thickened.

Meanwhile, preheat oven to 190C (375F/Gas 5). Return meat, kidneys and onion to pan, stir well, then spoon on top of pizza, reserving a little sauce. Bake in the oven for 15 minutes, spoon over reserved sauce and cook for a further 5 minutes. Serve at once, garnished with thyme.

Serves 4-6.

ORIENTAL CHICKEN PIZZA

1 quantity Traditional Pizza Dough, made up to end of step 2, see pages 10 and 11

TOPPING:

2 skinned, boneless chicken breasts

1 onion, finely chopped

2 cloves garlic, crushed

2 tablespoons soy sauce

1 tablespoon lemon juice

2 teaspoons brown sugar

125 g (4 oz) soya beansprouts, trimmed

SAUCE:

155 g (5 oz) creamed coconut

440 ml (14 fl oz/1¾ cups) boiling water

1 teaspoon coriander seeds

1 teaspoon cumin seeds

2 cloves garlic, crushed

125 g (4 oz/½ cup) crunchy peanut butter

1 teaspoon brown sugar

1 fresh green chilli, seeded and finely chopped

3 tablespoons lemon juice

spring onion, parsley and cucumber, to garnish

Make the topping. Cut chicken into matchstick strips. Place in a glass bowl. Add onion, garlic, soy sauce, lemon juice, sugar and beansprouts. Mix well; let stand for 20 minutes.

Make the sauce. Mix coconut and boiling water together. Set aside. Crush spices, put in a pan; heat gently. Stir in rest of sauce ingredients, cover and cook gently for 10 minutes.

Meanwhile, preheat oven to 190C (375F/Gas 5). Grease a baking sheet. Knock back risen dough and knead briefly. Put dough in centre of baking sheet and press out to edges with knuckles. Pinch up edges to create a rim. Spoon chicken mixture on top of dough. Bake for 15-20 minutes until golden. Garnish and serve with the sauce.

Serves 4.

FRENCH BRIE PIZZA

1 quantity Traditional Pizza Dough, with walnuts, shaped and ready for topping, see pages 10 and 11

TOPPING:

2 small leeks, finely shredded

2 tablespoons walnut or olive oil

salt

250 g (8 oz) Brie or Camembert cheese

1 teaspoon green peppercorns in brine, drained

15 g (½ oz/2 tablespoons) chopped walnuts

Preheat oven to 220C (425F/Gas 7). Make the topping. Put leeks in a saucepan with 1 tablespoon oil. Cook gently for 5 minutes, stirring until soft. Brush dough with remaining oil, then spoon over the leeks. Season to taste with salt.

Slice cheese thinly, arrange over leeks. Lightly crush some or all of the peppercorns and sprinkle over leeks. Scatter walnuts over top. Bake in the oven for 20 minutes until dough is crisp and golden.

Serves 4.

— SAUSAGE & BEER PIZZA —

1 quantity Deep Pan Pizza Dough, shaped and ready for topping, see page 14

TOPPING:

1 tablespoon vegetable oil

½ teaspoon caraway seeds, if desired

30 g (1 oz/6 teaspoons) butter

1 onion, sliced

1 quantity Cheese Topping, see page 35, using 155 ml (5 fl oz/⅔ cup) lager instead of milk and 1 tablespoon German mustard instead of dry mustard

250 g (8 oz) smoked pork sausage, in one piece

1 tablespoon chopped fresh parsley

tomato slices and chopped parsley, to garnish

Preheat oven to 220C (425F/Gas 7). Brush dough with oil. Sprinkle with caraway seeds, if desired. Melt butter in a saucepan. Cook onion gently for 5 minutes until soft.

Spoon over dough. Spoon Cheese Topping over. Slice sausage into 1 cm (½ in) slices. Arrange over surface. Sprinkle with chopped parsley and bake in the oven for 20 minutes until dough is well risen and golden. Serve the pizza garnished with tomato slices and chopped parsley.

Serves 4.

– SOUR CREAM CAVIAR PIZZAS –

1 quantity Traditional Pizza Dough, made up to end of step 2, see pages 10 and 11
1 tablespoon vegetable oil
TO SERVE:
thick sour cream or natural yogurt
caviar, lumpfish or salmon roe
lemon slices
chopped fresh chives
quails' eggs, hard-boiled, if desired

Knock back risen dough and knead briefly. Divide into 20 equal pieces. Roll out each on a lightly floured surface to a circle measuring 7.5 cm (3 in). Cover with a clean cloth and allow to rise slightly.

Preheat oven to 200 C (400F/Gas 6). Grease 2 baking sheets. Arrange pizzas on baking sheets and brush with oil. Bake in the oven for 15 minutes.

Serve warm, topped with thick sour cream or yogurt, caviar, lumpfish or salmon roe, lemon, chives and sliced hard-boiled quails' eggs, if desired.

Serves 6.

GREEK SESAME PIZZA

1 quantity Traditional Pizza Dough, shaped and ready for topping, see pages 10 and 11
1 tablespoon vegetable oil
½ teaspoon dried oregano
TOPPING:
500 g (1 lb) frozen chopped spinach, thawed
2 tablespoons vegetable oil
1 bunch spring onions, finely chopped
1 clove garlic, crushed
125 g (4 oz) feta cheese, crumbled
125 g (4 oz/1 cup) cottage cheese
salt and pepper
1 egg, beaten
1 tablespoon sesame seeds
extra feta cheese, finely sliced, and cucumber and olives, to garnish

Preheat oven to 200 C (400F/Gas 6). Brush dough with oil and sprinkle with oregano.

Make the topping. Squeeze spinach well to remove excess water. In a saucepan, heat oil. Add spring onions and garlic. Cook, stirring, for 2 minutes. Add spinach and cheeses; stir well. Season to taste with salt and pepper.

Stir in beaten egg, then spread mixture over dough. Sprinkle with sesame seeds and bake in the oven for 20 minutes until filling is set and dough is crisp and golden. Garnish with cheese, cucumber and olives.

Serves 4.

MIDDLE EASTERN PIZZA

1 quantity Wholemeal Pizza Dough, shaped and ready for topping, see pages 10 and 11

TOPPING:

500 g (1 lb) minced beef

1 tablespoon olive oil

1 onion, finely chopped

1 clove garlic, crushed

1 teaspoon ground allspice

1 teaspoon ground cumin

salt and pepper

2 tablespoons tomato purée (paste)

155 ml (5 fl oz/²⁄₃ cup) stock

60 g (2 oz/½ cup) dried apricots, chopped finely

2 tablespoons chopped fresh coriander

juice of 1 lemon or lime

30 g (1 oz/2 tablespoons) pine nuts

1 tablespoon sesame seeds

lime slices and coriander sprigs, to garnish

TO SERVE:

natural yogurt

Preheat oven to 190C (375F/Gas 5). In a saucepan, cook minced beef with the olive oil, onion and garlic until brown, stirring occasionally to prevent lumps of meat forming.

Stir in the allspice, cumin, salt and pepper to taste, tomato purée (paste) and stock. Cover; cook for 10 minutes, stirring occasionally.

Stir the chopped dried apricots, chopped coriander, lemon or lime juice and pine nuts into the meat mixture. Spoon the mixture over the dough and sprinkle sesame seeds over the top. Bake in the oven for 20 minutes until the dough is crisp and golden.

Garnish with lime slices and sprigs of coriander and serve at once with natural yogurt.

Serves 4-6.

PIZZA WITH CLAMS

1 quantity Wholemeal Pizza Dough,
shaped and ready for topping, see pages 10
and 11

TOPPING:

500 g (1 lb) clams in the shell or 440 g
(14 oz) can clams in juice

3 tablespoons olive oil

1 quantity Tomato Topping, see page 19

salt and pepper

few drops chilli sauce

2 tablespoons chopped fresh parsley

Preheat oven to 220C (425F/Gas 7). If using clams in the shell, wash well and place in a saucepan with 1 tablespoon oil. Cover and cook over gentle heat until all the shells open. Remove from heat; strain pan juices into a bowl. Reserve.

Remove clams from their shells, reserving a few intact for garnishing. Place shelled clams in reserved juice.

Spread Tomato Topping over pizza dough. Sprinkle with remaining oil. Season to taste with salt and pepper, a sprinkling of chilli sauce and 1 tablespoon chopped parsley. Bake in the oven for 15 minutes. Spoon the shelled clams (or canned clams) and a little clam juice over pizza; cook for a further 5 minutes. Arrange reserved clams in shells on top. Sprinkle the pizza with remaining chopped parsley and serve at once.

Serves 4.

MEXICAN CHILLI PIZZA

1 quantity Cornmeal Pizza Dough, made up to end of step 2, see pages 10 and 11

TOPPING:

500 g (1 lb) minced beef

1 onion, chopped

1 clove garlic, crushed

salt and pepper

1 teaspoon ground cumin

1 teaspoon chilli powder

2 teaspoons tomato purée (paste)

432 g (15.25 oz) can kidney beans, drained

3 tomatoes, chopped

220 g (7 oz) can sweetcorn, drained

1 green pepper (capsicum), chopped

4-6 spring onions, chopped

60 g (2 oz/½ cup) grated Cheddar cheese

GUACAMOLE:

2 ripe avocados

juice of 1 lemon

salt and pepper

3 spring onions

few drops Tabasco sauce

Preheat oven to 220C (425F/Gas 7). Grease a 23 x 35.5 cm (10 x 14 in) Swiss roll tin. Knock back risen dough; knead briefly and place in centre of tin. Press out to sides; pinch up edges to create a rim.

In a saucepan, cook beef, onion and garlic until meat browns. Season. Add spices and tomato purée (paste). Cook for 10 minutes.

Rinse and mash kidney beans. Stir in any juices from cooked meat. Spread beans over dough. Spoon meat mixture on top.

Arrange tomatoes, sweetcorn and green pepper (capsicum) in circles on top of pizza. Place spring onions in centre. Sprinkle with cheese. Bake in the oven for 20 minutes until golden. Serve with guacamole made by mixing all ingredients smoothly in a blender.

Serves 6-8.

CURRY PIZZA

1 quantity Traditional Pizza Dough, shaped and ready for topping, see pages 10 and 11

1 tablespoon sesame seeds

TOPPING:

250 g (8 oz) potatoes, cooked

2 tablespoons vegetable oil

1 onion, finely chopped

90 g (3 oz) frozen peas, thawed

2.5 cm (1 in) piece fresh root ginger, peeled and grated

1 small green chilli, seeded and chopped

1 tablespoon chopped fresh coriander

1/2 teaspoon ground cumin

1/2 teaspoon ground coriander

1/2 teaspoon garam masala

salt and pepper

2 tablespoon lemon juce

TO SERVE:

yogurt and onion salad

Make the topping. Cut potatoes into small cubes. Heat oil in a saucepan, add onion; cook, stirring, for 5 minutes. Add potatoes, peas, ginger, chilli, coriander, 2 tablespoons water and spices. Cook, stirring, for 5 minutes, adding more water if mixture becomes too dry. Season to taste with salt and pepper; add lemon juice. Leave to stand for about 20 minutes.

Preheat oven to 220 C (425F/Gas 7). Spread mixture over the dough, sprinkle with sesame seeds, then bake in the oven for 20 minutes until the dough is crisp and golden. Serve with yogurt and onion salad.

Serves 4.

PISSALADIÈRE

1 quantity Traditional Pizza Dough,
shaped and ready for topping, see pages 10
and 11

TOPPING:

440 g (14 oz) can crushed tomatoes

1 onion, chopped

1 clove garlic, crushed

2 tablespoons olive oil

1 tablespoon chopped fresh parsley

2 teaspoons chopped fresh thyme or 1
teaspoon dried thyme

1 tablespoon tomato purée (paste)

1 egg

60 g (2 oz/½ cup) grated Gruyère
cheese

salt and pepper

90 g (3 oz) can anchovy fillets

black olives

thyme sprigs and Gruyère cheese, to
garnish, if desired

Make the topping. In a saucepan, heat tomatoes, onion, garlic, 1 tablespoon oil, parsley, thyme and tomato purée (paste) together. Bring to the boil, reduce heat; simmer 30 minutes. Cool slightly.

Preheat oven to 200 C (400F/Gas 6). Brush dough with remaining oil.

Beat egg and stir into tomato mixture with grated cheese. Spread over dough. Season to taste with salt and pepper. Drain and cut anchovy fillets in thin strips. Arrange in a lattice over pizza. Add olives and bake in the oven for 20 minutes until dough is crisp and golden. Serve garnished with thyme and Gruyère cheese, if desired.

Serves 4.

SPANISH PIZZA

1 quantity Traditional Pizza Dough, shaped and ready for topping, see pages 10 and 11

TOPPING:

3 skinned chicken breast (fillets), cooked

1 tablespoon olive oil

1 onion, chopped

60 g (2 oz) streaky bacon, chopped

185 g (6 oz/1¼ cups) long-grain rice

125 ml (4 fl oz/½ cup) dry white wine

125 ml (4 fl oz/½ cup) chicken stock

salt and pepper

1 red pepper (capsicum), seeded and chopped

125 g (4 oz) chorizo or garlic sausage, sliced

4 tomatoes, seeded and chopped

few strands saffron, if desired

parsley and chopped pepper (capsicum), to garnish

Make the topping. Cut the chicken into cubes and set aside. In a saucepan, heat oil, add the onion and bacon and fry for 5 minutes. Add rice, wine and stock and season. Bring to the boil, cover and cook for 5 minutes.

Add pepper (capsicum), chorizo or garlic sausage, tomatoes and saffron, if desired. Stir, then cook for 12-15 minutes until rice is tender and most of the liquid has reduced. Stir in chicken.

Meanwhile, preheat oven to 220C (425F/Gas 7). Spoon topping on top of the dough, then bake in the oven for 20 minutes. Serve garnished with parsley and pepper (capsicum).

Serves 6.

SWISS CHEESE PIZZA

1 quantity Traditional Pizza Dough,
shaped and ready for topping, see pages 10
and 11

1 tablespoon vegetable oil

TOPPING:

1 clove garlic, chopped

185 g (6 oz/1½ cups) grated Cheddar
cheese

185 g (6 oz/1½ cups) grated Gruyère
cheese

2 tablespoons kirsch

freshly grated nutmeg

pepper

red pimento and oregano sprigs,
to garnish

Preheat oven to 220C (425F/Gas
7). Brush dough with oil and
sprinkle dough with garlic and
grated cheeses. Sprinkle with
kirsch, nutmeg and pepper. Bake in
the oven for 20 minutes until dough
is crisp and golden.

Serve the pizza garnished with
pimento strips and oregano sprigs.

Serves 6-8.

Variation: Substitute the same
quantity of Emmental cheese for
the Gruyère cheese, if preferred.

DIM SUM PIZZA

1 quantity Traditional Pizza Dough, made up to end of step 2, see pages 10 and 11

FILLING:

250 g (8 oz) minced pork

2 tablespoons vegetable oil

1 bunch spring onions, chopped

250 g (8 oz) peeled prawns, thawed if frozen

125 g (4 oz) mushrooms, finely chopped

1 tablespoon black bean sauce

TO SERVE:

soy sauce

spring onion tassels and carrot flowers

Knock back risen dough and knead briefly. Divide into 12 equal pieces. Roll out on a lightly floured surface to circles measuring approximately 7.5 cm (3 in). Cover with a clean cloth while preparing filling.

In a saucepan, fry pork in the oil with spring onions for 4 minutes, stirring. Remove from heat, stir in prawns, mushrooms and sauce. Place 1 tablespoon of filling in the centre of a circle of dough. Dampen edges with water, gather together in the centre and pinch together. Repeat with remaining dough and filling.

Line trays of a tiered, bamboo steamer with oiled greaseproof paper. Arrange dim sum on paper and steam over boiling water for 30 minutes until well risen and firm.

Serve hot with soy sauce for dipping, garnished with spring onion tassels and carrot flowers.

Serves 6.

MUSHROOM CALZONI

1 quantity Traditional Pizza Dough, made to end of step 2, see pages 10 and 11

1 tablespoon olive oil

beaten egg, to glaze

grated Parmesan cheese and oregano sprigs, to garnish

FILLING:

500 g (1 lb) open mushrooms, sliced

2 tablespoons olive oil

1 clove garlic, sliced

salt and pepper

½ teaspoon dried oregano

250 g (8 oz) ricotta or curd cheese

2 tablespoons freshly grated Parmesan cheese

Make the filling. In a saucepan, cook mushrooms in oil with garlic for 3-4 minutes. Remove with a slotted spoon and place in a bowl. Season to taste with salt and pepper; add oregano. Mix in ricotta or curd cheese and Parmesan.

Preheat oven to 220C (425F/ Gas 7). Grease 2 baking sheets. Divide dough into 2 equal pieces. Roll out both pieces on a lightly floured surface to circles measuring 25 cm (10 in) in diameter. Brush lightly with oil.

Divide filling between the 2 pieces of dough, confining it to one half of each circle. Dampen edges with water, then fold over dough to enclose filling and seal well by pressing with a fork. Transfer to baking sheets, brush with beaten egg and make 2 or 3 air holes with a sharp knife. Bake in the oven for 20 minutes until golden. Garnish with grated Parmesan cheese and sprigs of oregano.

Serves 4-6.

LEEK & ONION CALZONI

1 quantity Traditional Pizza dough, made up to end of step 2, see pages 10 and 11

1 tablespoon olive oil

beaten egg, to glaze

leek, onion and olive slices, to garnish

FILLING:

3 tablespoons olive oil

2 small leeks, sliced

2 onions, sliced

1 large Spanish onion, sliced

125 ml (4 fl oz/½ cup) dry white wine

125 ml (4 fl oz/½ cup) single (light) cream

salt and pepper

freshly grated nutmeg, to taste

125 g (4 oz) stuffed olives, chopped

Make filling. Heat oil and cook leeks and onions gently for 10 minutes until soft. Increase heat, add wine and cook until almost dry.

Reduce heat, add cream and season to taste with salt, pepper and nutmeg. Cook for 2-3 minutes until creamy. Remove from heat, stir in olives and set aside.

Preheat oven to 220C (425F/Gas 7). Grease 2 baking sheets. Divide dough into 2 equal pieces. Roll out both pieces on a lightly floured surface to circles measuring 25 cm (10 in) in diameter. Brush lightly with oil.

Divide filling between the 2 pieces of dough, confining it to one half of each circle. Dampen edges with water, then fold over dough to enclose filling and seal well by pressing with a fork. Transfer to baking sheets, brush with beaten egg and make 2 or 3 air holes with a sharp knife. Bake in the oven for 20 minutes until golden. Serve garnished with leek, onion and olive slices.

Serves 4-6.

CHICKEN LIVER CALZONI

1 quantity Traditional Pizza Dough, made up to end of step 2, see pages 10 and 11
1 tablespoon vegetable oil
beaten egg, to glaze
sage leaves, to garnish
FILLING:
60 g (2 oz/¼ cup) butter
500 g (1 lb) chicken livers, trimmed
6 rashers streaky bacon, chopped
1 tablespoon chopped fresh sage
750 g (1½ lb) fresh spinach, trimmed
salt and pepper
few drops lemon juice
freshly grated nutmeg, to taste

Make the filling. In a saucepan, melt butter and cook chicken livers quickly until brown but still pink on the inside. Remove with slotted spoon and reserve.

Add bacon to saucepan, cook until brown. Remove with slotted spoon and add to livers with sage. Add spinach to saucepan. Cover and cook until wilted. Drain well, then chop roughly. Season to taste with salt and pepper, lemon juice and nutmeg.

Preheat oven to 220C (425F/Gas 7). Grease 2 baking sheets. Divide dough into 2 equal pieces. Roll out both pieces on a lightly floured surface to circles measuring 25 cm (10 in) in diameter. Brush lightly with oil.

Divide filling between the 2 pieces of dough, confining it to one half of each circle. Dampen edges with water, then fold over dough to enclose filling and seal well by pressing with a fork. Transfer to baking sheets, brush with beaten egg and make 2 or 3 air holes with a sharp knife. Bake in the oven for 20 minutes until golden. Serve garnished with sage leaves.

Serves 4-6.

BROCCOLI CALZONI

1 quantity Deep Pan Pizza Dough, made up to end of step 1, see page 14

1 teaspoon dried dill weed

1 tablespoon olive oil

beaten egg, to glaze

chopped fresh dill, to garnish

FILLING:

375 g (12 oz) broccoli

250 g (8 oz/2 cups) grated Cheddar cheese

salt and pepper

In a saucepan of boiling water, blanch broccoli for 2 minutes. Drain and refresh with cold water. Drain again. Chop coarsely.

Preheat oven to 220C (425F/Gas 7). Grease 2 baking sheets. Knead dough with dill weed until evenly distributed. Divide into 2 equal pieces. Roll out each piece on a lightly floured surface to a circle measuring 25 cm (10 in) in diameter. Brush lightly with oil.

Divide broccoli between the 2 pieces of dough, confining it to one half of each circle. Sprinkle with two-thirds of the cheese and season with salt and pepper. Dampen edges with water, fold over dough to enclose filling and seal well by pressing with a fork. Transfer to baking sheets, brush with beaten egg and sprinkle with remaining cheese. Make 2 or 3 air holes with a sharp knife. Bake in the oven for 20 minutes until golden. Serve the calzoni garnished with a little chopped fresh dill.

Serves 4-6.

—— WATERCRESS PIZZA ROLLS ——

1 quantity Deep Pan Pizza Dough, made
up to end of step 1, see page 14

watercress sprigs, to garnish

FILLING:

30 g (1 oz/6 teaspoons) butter

1 onion, finely chopped

3 bunches watercress, finely chopped

250 g (8 oz) cottage cheese

3 tablespoons grated Parmesan cheese

1 tablespoon lemon juice

1 egg, beaten

salt and pepper

Make the filling. In a saucepan,
melt butter and cook onion for 5
minutes until soft. Add chopped
watercress and cook for a further 3
minutes. Remove from heat, stir in
cottage cheese, 2 tablespoons
Parmesan cheese, lemon juice and
beaten egg. Season to taste with salt
and pepper. Cool and chill until
firm.

Grease a baking sheet. Roll out
dough on a lightly floured surface to
a rectangle measuring about 25 x
35.5 cm (10 x 14 in).

Spread filling evenly over dough
leaving a small border clear. Roll up
from the long sides to make a firm
roll. Seal edges well. Cut into 8-10
slices and arrange on baking sheet.
Cover with plastic wrap and leave
to rise for about 30 minutes.

Meanwhile, preheat oven to
220C (425F/Gas 7). Sprinkle rolls
with remaining Parmesan cheese.
Bake in the oven for 20 minutes
until dough is crisp and golden.
Garnish with watercress.

Serves 4-6.

PIZZA PIPERADE

1 quantity Cornmeal Pizza Dough, made up to end of step 2, see pages 10 and 11

TOPPING:

6 eggs

salt and pepper

1 orange pepper (capsicum), halved and seeded

1 yellow pepper (capsicum), halved and seeded

2 large or 4 small spring onions

1 tablespoon olive oil

2 tablespoons chopped fresh parsley

pepper (capsicum) rings and parsley sprigs, to garnish

Preheat oven to 200C (400F/Gas 6). Grease a 25 cm (10 in) deep pan pizza tin. Knock back dough, knead briefly on a lightly floured surface.

Place dough in centre of tin, press out to sides with the knuckles.

Beat the eggs together in a bowl with salt and pepper to taste. Set the mixture aside.

Slice peppers (capsicums) into strips, slice spring onions thickly. Heat oil in a saucepan, add peppers and onions and cook for 3 minutes, stirring constantly. Spoon on top of dough. Pour egg mixture on top. Sprinkle with chopped parsley. Bake in the oven for 20 minutes until the egg mixture is set and golden. Serve at once, garnished with pepper (capsicum) rings and parsley sprigs.

Serves 4.

PIZZA RING

1 quantity Traditional Pizza Dough, made up to end of step 2, see pages 10 and 11

60 g (2 oz/½ cup) freshly grated Parmesan cheese

salt and pepper

FILLING:

75 g (2½ oz) pepper salami, sliced

45 g (1½ oz) smoked cheese

75 g (2½ oz) Mozzarella cheese

45 g (1½ oz) Gruyère cheese

4 slices processed Cheddar cheese

2 hard-boiled eggs

1 tablespoon olive oil

lettuce leaves and cherry tomatoes, to garnish

Grease 22.5 cm (9 in) ring tin. Knock back risen dough, then knead dough with Parmesan cheese and salt and pepper to taste. Roll out on a lightly floured surface to a rectangle measuring 25 x 35.5 cm (10 x 14 in). Chop salami and all the cheeses into small pieces. Mix together.

Sprinkle over surface of dough, leaving a narrow border clear. Halve eggs and cut each half into 3. Arrange in lines from top to bottom across the length of dough. Roll up from the long side and seal edges well.

Coil into a circle and seal ends together. Fit into ring tin. Cover with plastic wrap and leave to stand for 1 hour until dough has risen to just below top of tin. Brush with oil.

Preheat oven to 220C (425F/Gas 7). Bake ring in the oven for 45 minutes until well risen and golden. Serve cold, garnished with lettuce leaves and cherry tomatoes.

Serves 6.

SALMON CALZONCELLI

1 quantity Traditional Pizza Dough, made up to end of step 2, see pages 10 and 11

TOPPING:

125 g (4 oz) cream cheese

250 g (8 oz) thinly sliced smoked salmon

pepper

juice of ½ lemon

lemon and chives, to garnish

Preheat oven to 200 C (400F/Gas 6). Grease 2 baking sheets. Knock back risen dough and knead briefly. Roll out on a lightly floured surface to 0.3 cm (⅛ in) thick. Using a 7.5 cm (3 in) cutter, cut out as many circles as possible. Keep covered with clean cloth while re-rolling dough and cutting out more to make 10-15 in total.

In a bowl, mix cream cheese and smoked salmon together with pepper and lemon juice. Place 1 teaspoon of mixture on one half of each circle. Dampen edges with water, fold over to enclose filling and seal well by pressing with a fork. Transfer to baking sheets and bake for 10-15 minutes until golden. Serve hot or cold, garnished with lemon and chives.

Serves 10-15.

HAM & SALAMI CALZONCELLI

1 quantity Traditional Pizza Dough, made up to end of step 2, see pages 10 and 11
cress and radish slices, to garnish
FILLING:
60 g (2 oz) sliced ham
60 g (2 oz) sliced salami
60 g (2 oz) Mozzarella cheese
2 tablespoons chopped fresh parsley
1 tablespoon freshly grated Parmesan cheese
1 egg, beaten
salt and pepper

Preheat oven to 200C (400F/Gas 6). Grease 2 baking sheets. Knock back risen dough and knead briefly. Roll out and cut dough as for Salmon Calzoncelli, see page 89.

Chop ham and salami very finely. Place in a bowl. Grate Mozzarella cheese and put in bowl with parsley and Parmesan cheese. Stir in egg and season to taste with salt and pepper. Mix thoroughly.

Place 1 teaspoon of the mixture on one half of each circle. Dampen edges with water, then fold over to enclose filling and seal well by pressing with a fork. Transfer to baking sheets and bake for 15 minutes until golden. Serve hot or cold, garnished with cress and radish slices.

Serves 10-15.

Variation: Chop 90 g (3 oz) mushrooms finely and mix with 6 tablespoons Tomato Topping, see page 19, and 1 tablespoon freshly grated Parmesan cheese. Use as the filling.

LEAFY GREEN CALZONI

1 quantity Traditional Pizza Dough, made up to end of step 2, see pages 10 and 11

beaten egg, to glaze

tomato slices and marjoram sprigs, to garnish

FILLING:

500 g (1 lb) cabbage or spring greens

3 tablespoons olive oil

2 onions, chopped

440 g (14 oz) can tomatoes, drained

2 cloves garlic, crushed

½ teaspoon dried oregano

salt and pepper

Trim and discard hard stalks from cabbage or spring greens. Wash well and cook in a large saucepan (with just the water that clings to the leaves) for 10-15 minutes until tender. Drain well and chop finely.

Heat 2 tablespoons oil in a saucepan; cook onions until soft. Chop tomatoes, add to pan with garlic and oregano and salt and pepper to taste.

Cook for 20 minutes until thick.

Preheat oven to 220C (425F/Gas 7). Grease 2 baking sheets. Knock back risen dough and knead briefly. Divide dough into 2 equal pieces. Roll out both pieces on a lightly floured surface to circles measuring 25 cm (10 in) in diameter. Lightly brush with remaining oil.

Mix tomato mixture with the cooked greens. Divide between the 2 pieces of dough, confining mixture to one half of each circle. Dampen edges with water. Fold dough over to cover filling and seal well by pressing with a fork. Place on baking sheets, brush with beaten egg and make 2 or 3 air holes with a sharp knife. Bake for 20 minutes until golden. Cut in half. Serve hot, garnished with tomato and marjoram.

Serves 4.

COUNTRY CALZONI

1 quantity Traditional Pizza Dough, made up to end of step 2, see pages 10 and 11

2 tablespoons olive oil

mushroom slices and thyme sprigs, to garnish

FILLING:

4 large pork sausages with herbs

315 g (10 oz) goat's cheese, such as Chèvre

6-8 dried tomatoes in oil, see Note

125 g (4 oz) mushrooms, sliced

2 dried red chillies, crushed

beaten egg, to glaze

Preheat oven to 220C (425F/Gas 7). Grease 2 baking sheets. Knock back risen dough and knead briefly. Divide dough into 2 equal pieces. Roll both out on a lightly floured surface to circles measuring 25 cm (10 in) in diameter. Brush lightly with oil.

Remove skin from sausages and discard. Break sausagemeat into small pieces and sprinkle over both circles of dough, confining it to one half of circle. Chop cheese roughly and sprinkle over sausagemeat. Cut dried tomatoes into pieces and sprinkle over with mushrooms and crushed chillies.

Fold over dough to enclose filling, dampen edges with water and seal well by pressing with a fork. Transfer to baking sheets, brush with beaten egg and make 2 or 3 air holes with a sharp knife. Bake in the oven for 20 minutes until golden. Serve garnished with mushrooms and thyme.

Serves 4.

Note: Dried tomatoes in oil are available from Italian food shops and delicatessens.

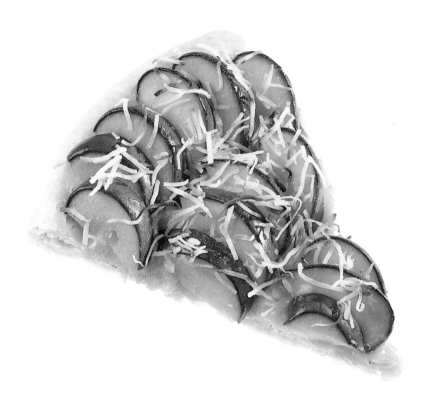

PLUM PIZZA

1 quantity Deep Pan Pizza Dough, made up to end of step 1, see page 14

CUSTARD TOPPING:

7 teaspoons custard powder

4½ teaspoons sugar

315 ml (10 fl oz/1¼ cups) milk

625 g (1¼ lb) plums, halved and stoned

2 tablespoons shredded coconut

TO SERVE:

whipped cream

Preheat oven to 220C (425F/Gas 7). Grease a deep pan pizza tin. Place dough in centre, press to edges with the knuckles, then cover and leave to rise until halfway up the tin.

Meanwhile, make topping. In a bowl, blend custard powder and sugar with a little of the milk until smooth. Heat remaining milk until nearly boiling. Stir into custard powder, then return to pan. Bring to the boil, stirring until thickened. Remove from heat and leave to cool a little.

Slice plum halves into 4 sections. Spoon custard on top of dough. Arrange plum slices on top and sprinkle with coconut. Bake in the oven for 20 minutes. Serve hot or cold with cream.

Serves 4-6.

CHOC-TRUFFLE PIZZA

1 quantity Traditional Pizza Dough, made up to end of step 3, see page 14

TOPPING:

1 quantity Custard Topping, see page 93

90 g (3 oz) plain chocolate, melted

250 g (8 oz) plain sponge cake crumbs

1 tablespoon apricot jam

90 g (3 oz) white chocolate, melted

60 g (2 oz/½ cup) finely chopped almonds

white chocolate curls, to decorate

Preheat oven to 220C (425F/Gas 7). Bake dough in the oven for 20 minutes until golden. Cool.

Meanwhile, make topping. In a bowl, combine custard and melted dark chocolate. Chill until firm.

Make truffles, combine cake crumbs, jam and white chocolate in a bowl until a stiff paste is formed. Divide mixture into small balls and roll in the chopped almonds to coat.

To assemble pizza, spread chocolate-flavoured custard on top of pizza and arrange truffles around the edge. Sprinkle with white chocolate curls.

Serves 6.

— RASPBERRY MALLOW PIZZA —

1 quantity Crumble Pizza Dough, made up
to end of step 3, see page 15

TOPPING:

3 tablespoons raspberry jam

500 g (1 lb) raspberries

185 g (6 oz) packet marshmallows

few raspberries and raspberry leaves to
decorate, if desired

Preheat oven to 200C (400F/Gas
6). Bake pizza base in the oven for 5
minutes. Remove from oven,
reduce temperature to 180C (350F/
Gas 4).

In a bowl, beat jam until soft.
Spread over pizza base. Spoon over
raspberries. Arrange marshmallows
over the raspberries. Bake in the
oven for 15-20 minutes until soft.
Allow to cool before serving,
decorated with raspberries and
raspberry leaves, if desired.

Serves 6-8.

TROPICAL PIZZA

1 quantity Traditional Pizza Dough, made up to end of step 3, see pages 10 and 11

TOPPING:

250 g (8 oz) fresh dates

125 g (4 oz) cream cheese

1 small pineapple

2 kiwi fruit

Preheat oven to 200C (400F/Gas 6). Prick dough with a fork, then bake in the oven for 20 minutes until golden. Leave to cool.

Meanwhile, halve and stone dates. Reserve a few for decoration, then chop the remainder and put in a bowl with the cream cheese. Mix well, then set aside.

Cut top and base from pineapple, then cut off skin. Halve pineapple, slice thinly and cut out hard central core. Peel kiwi fruit; slice thinly.

Spread cream cheese on top of pizza. Arrange slices of pineapple and kiwi on top. Decorate with reserved date halves. Chill until ready to serve.

Serves 6.

BERRY STREUSEL PIZZA

1 quantity Traditional Pizza Dough, made up to end of step 3, see pages 10 and 11

TOPPING:

125 g (4 oz/1 cup) self-raising flour

90 g (3 oz/⅓ cup) caster sugar

90 g (3 oz/⅓ cup) butter

1 teaspoon ground cinnamon

1 quantity Custard Topping, see page 93

500 g (1 lb) bottled or canned gooseberries, drained

TO SERVE:

cream

Preheat oven to 200C (400F/Gas 6). Prick dough with a fork and bake in the oven for 20 minutes until golden. Allow to cool slightly.

In a bowl, mix flour and sugar, rub in butter until mixture resembles breadcrumbs. Stir in cinnamon and 2 tablespoons water and mix with a fork until a lumpy texture is obtained.

Spoon custard on top of pizza, top with gooseberries, then sprinkle crumble topping over the top. Bake in the oven for 10-15 minutes until light golden. Serve hot with cream.

Serves 6.

— CHERRY & ALMOND PIZZA —

1 quantity Traditional Pizza Dough, made up to end of step 2, see pages 10 and 11

30 g (1 oz/2 tablespoons) ground almonds

TOPPING:

2 egg whites

125 g (4 oz/¾ cup) ground almonds

90 g (3 oz/⅓ cup) caster sugar

few drops almond essence

750 g (1½ lb) jar Morello cherries in juice

60 g (2 oz/½ cup) flaked almonds

3 tablespoons Morello cherry jam

icing sugar for dusting

whipped cream, to decorate

Preheat oven to 220C (425F/Gas 7). Knock back risen dough and knead dough with ground almonds. Follow instructions given in step 3, see page 10.

In a bowl, lightly whisk egg whites. Stir in ground almonds, caster sugar and almond essence. Spread the mixture evenly over pizza base.

Drain cherries, reserving juice. Spoon over pizza, reserving a few for decoration. Sprinkle with flaked almonds and bake in the oven for 20 minutes until dough is crisp and golden.

Meanwhile, in a saucepan, heat reserved juice and jam until syrupy. Dust cooked pizza with icing sugar and decorate with whipped cream and reserved cherries. Serve the sauce separately.

Serves 4-6.

APPLE PIE PIZZA

1 quantity Crumble Pizza Dough, made up to end of step 3, see page 15

TOPPING:

3 tablespoons apple and pear spread, see Note

2 tablespoons apple juice or water

3 cooking apples, peeled and cored

60 g (2 oz/2 tablespoons) sultanas

60 g (2 oz/½ cup) chopped walnuts

60 g (2 oz/⅓ cup) soft brown sugar

1 teaspoon ground cinnamon

125 g (4 oz) marzipan

TO SERVE:

apple slices and whipped cream

Preheat oven to 200 C (400F/Gas 6). Bake pizza base in the oven for 10 minutes. Remove from oven and then reduce the oven temperature to 180 C (350F/Gas 4).

Mix apple and pear spread with apple juice or water to form a soft paste. Spread over pizza base. Slice apples thinly. Place in a bowl with the sultanas, walnuts, sugar and cinnamon. Mix well. Spoon over dough and level surface. Grate marzipan and sprinkle over surface. Bake in the oven for 25-30 minutes. Serve with apple slices and whipped cream.

Serves 6.

Note: Apple and pear spread (called Apple butter in America) is available from most good health food shops.

LEMON MERINGUE PIZZA

1 quantity Traditional Pizza Dough, made up to end of step 3, see pages 10 and 11

TOPPING:

9 teaspoons cornflour

juice and grated peel 2 lemons

220 g (7 oz/1 cup) caster sugar

2 eggs, separated

star fruit and lemon balm, to decorate

Preheat oven to 200C (400F/Gas 6). Prick dough with a fork and bake in the oven for 20 minutes until golden. Leave to cool slightly. Reduce oven temperature to 180C (350F/Gas 4).

Make topping, place cornflour, lemon juice and peel in a saucepan with 100 ml (3½ fl oz/⅓ cup) water. Bring slowly to the boil, stirring until mixture thickens. Add 125 g (4 oz/½ cup) sugar and the egg yolks, then beat well. Spoon on top of pizza.

In a large bowl, whisk egg whites until stiff. Whisk in half of remaining sugar, then fold in the rest. Pipe or spoon on top of lemon mixture to cover filling completely. Bake in the oven for 10 minutes until meringue is golden. Serve decorated with slices of star fruit and lemon balm leaves.

Serves 6.

CHRISTMAS CALZONI

1 quantity Deep Pan Pizza Dough, made up to end of step 1, see page 14

icing sugar for dusting

FILLING:

125g (4 oz/½ cup) unsalted butter, softened

125 g (4 oz/¾ cup) icing sugar, sifted

125 g (4 oz/⅔ cup) soft brown sugar

1 tablespoon milk

1 tablespoon brandy

6 tablespoons mincemeat

Preheat oven to 220C (425F/Gas 7). Grease 2 baking sheets. Divide dough into 2 equal pieces. Roll out both pieces to circles measuring about 25 cm (10 in) in diameter.

Make the filling. In a bowl, beat butter and sugars together. Gradually stir in milk and brandy until mixture is light and fluffy.

Place 1 tablespoon brandy butter and 3 tablespoons mincemeat to one side of each circle of dough. Brush edges with water, fold over and seal edges firmly. Transfer to baking sheets and bake in the oven for 20 minutes until golden.

Dust with icing sugar. Serve warm with rest of brandy butter.

Serves 4-6.

PEAR & GINGER PIZZA

1 quantity Deep Pan Pizza Dough, shaped
and ready for topping, see page 14

TOPPING:

4 pears, peeled and cored

3 tablespoons apple and pear spread

60 g (2 oz/½ cup) chopped walnuts

2 tablespoons chopped crystallized ginger

60 g (1 oz/6 teaspoons) butter, melted

crystallized ginger and angelica, to
decorate

TO SERVE:

whipped cream

Preheat oven to 220 C (425F/Gas
7). Chop 2 pears and put in a bowl
with the apple and pear spread,
walnuts and ginger. Mix well, then
spread over the dough.

Halve remaining pears. With a
sharp knife, slice each half from the
rounded end to the point without
cutting right through. Fan out the
sections and arrange on top of the
pizza. Brush with melted butter.
Bake in the oven for 20 minutes.
Decorate with crystallized ginger
and angelica and serve with whipped cream.

Serves 4-6.

BANANA MAPLE SYRUP PIZZA

1 quantity Traditional Pizza Dough, made up to end of step 3, see pages 10 and 11

TOPPING:

30 g (1 oz/6 teaspoons) butter, melted

4 bananas

2-3 tablespoons maple syrup

60 g (2 oz/½ cup) chopped walnuts

TO SERVE:

whipped cream and maple syrup

Preheat oven to 220C (425F/Gas 7). Brush dough with melted butter.

In a bowl, mash 2 bananas with maple syrup. Spread over pizza base. Slice remaining bananas. Arrange over pizza. Brush with remaining melted butter. Bake in the oven for 20 minutes until dough is crisp and brown.

Sprinkle pizza with chopped walnuts and serve with whipped cream and maple syrup.

Serves 4-6.

ORANGE LIQUEUR PIZZA

1 quantity Deep Pan Pizza Dough, shaped and ready for topping, see page 14

TOPPING:

30 g (1 oz/6 teaspoons) butter, melted, for brushing

3 oranges

2 tablespoons orange liqueur

2 tablespoons orange marmalade

2 tablespoons soft brown sugar

bay leaves, to decorate

Preheat oven to 220C (425F/Gas 7). Brush dough with melted butter.

Using a canelle knife, remove strips of orange peel, set aside for decoration. Peel oranges thinly with a sharp knife or potato peeler. Cut off white pith and discard. Slice oranges thinly. Arrange over dough.

In a pan, heat liqueur, marmalade and sugar until syrupy. Spoon over pizza and bake in the oven for 20 minutes. Meanwhile, blanch peel strips in boiling water for 2-3 minutes. Drain and cool. Decorate pizza with orange peel strips and bay leaves.

Serves 4-6.

— BERRY CHEESECAKE PIZZA —

1 quantity Crumble Pizza Dough, made to end of step 3, see page 15

TOPPING:

500 g (1 lb) strawberries

375 g (12 oz) curd or low fat cheese

125 ml (4 fl oz/½ cup) milk

grated peel of ½ orange

4 tablespoons orange juice

2 tablespoons clear honey

1 egg, beaten

2 tablespoons redcurrant jelly

whipped cream and strawberry leaves, to decorate

Preheat oven to 190C (375F/Gas 5). Bake dough in the oven for 15 minutes. Meanwhile, hull and chop half the strawberries. In a bowl, blend curd or low fat cheese with milk, orange peel, orange juice, honey and egg.

Spoon chopped strawberries over pizza base. Spoon cheese mixture on top and smooth over. Bake in the oven for 35-40 minutes. Switch off the oven, open the door and allow the cheesecake to cool gradually.

In a saucepan, heat redcurrant jelly until melted. Arrange reserved strawberries on top of cheesecake. Brush with melted jelly. Serve decorated with whipped cream and strawberry leaves.

Serves 4-6.

PANETTONE

30 g (1 oz/6 teaspoons) fresh (compressed)
yeast, or 2 tablespoons dried active yeast

90 ml (3 fl oz/⅓ cup) hand-hot water

60 g (2 oz/⅓ cup) sugar

4 egg yolks

few drops vanilla essence

grated peel of 1 lemon

375 g (12 oz/3 cups) strong white flour

½ teaspoon salt

90 g (3 oz/⅓ cup) butter, softened

60 g (2 oz/⅓ cup) chopped candied peel

45 g (1½ oz/2 tablespoons) raisins

45 g (1½ oz/2 tablespoons) sultanas

60 g (2 oz/¼ cup) butter, melted, for
brushing

In a small bowl, cream fresh yeast with water; put in warm place until frothy. If using dried active yeast, whisk with 1 teaspoon of sugar and the water; leave until frothy.

In a large bowl, put sugar, egg yolks, essence and lemon peel. Stir in yeast mixture. Mix flour with salt. Gradually add two-thirds flour to yeast mixture, until a sticky dough is obtained.

Divide butter into 3 equal pieces. Add one piece at a time, kneading until mixture is heavy and stringy. Add remaining flour; mix well. Knead on a lightly floured surface until firm and oily, but not sticky. Place in a bowl. Cover, set aside for 1½ hours until doubled.

Preheat oven to 200C (400F/Gas 6). Well grease a charlotte tin. Knead peel, raisins and sultanas into dough. Place in tin, cover, leave to rise to just below top of tin.

Brush with melted butter; bake for 10 minutes. Reduce temperature to 180C (350F/Gas 4). Brush again with butter; bake for 30-40 minutes. Brush with more butter after 15 minutes. Leave to cool.

Serves 10-12.

GRAPE BREAD

1 quantity Deep Pan Pizza Dough, made up to end of step 1, see page 14

30 g (1 oz/5 teaspoons) caster sugar

FILLING:

375 g (12 oz) red seedless grapes

60 g (2 oz/¼ cup) caster sugar

TO SERVE:

extra sugar and pouring cream

Preheat oven to 220C (425F/Gas 7). Grease a 25 cm (10 in) deep pan pizza tin or sandwich tin.

Spread grapes on a baking sheet and bake in the oven for 10 minutes. Meanwhile knock back risen dough and knead with 30 g (1 oz/5 teaspoons) caster sugar. Divide into 2 equal pieces. Roll each piece to a circle measuring 25 cm (10 in) in diameter. Remove grapes from oven; turn off oven.

Place one dough circle in tin. Brush surface with water and spoon over half the grapes. Sprinkle with half the remaining sugar. Lay second piece of dough on top and press gently with fingertips to seal dough around grapes and make small pockets.

Spoon remaining grapes over the surface and sprinkle with remaining sugar. Cover with plastic wrap and leave to rise for 1½ hours. Preheat oven to 200C (400F/Gas 6). Bake in the oven for 20-25 minutes until golden. Cool, then dust with extra sugar and serve with cream.

Serves 4-6.

WALNUT BREAD

1 quantity Traditional Pizza Dough, made
up to end of step 2, see pages 10 and 11

155 g (5 oz/1¼ cups) chopped walnuts

vegetable oil for brushing

Grease a baking sheet. Knock back
risen dough and knead in walnuts.
Flatten to a round loaf shape about
25 cm (10 in) in diameter and place
on baking sheet. Cover with plastic
wrap and allow to stand for 1-1½
hours until doubled in size.

Preheat oven to 190 C (375F/Gas
5). Brush dough with oil. With a
sharp knife, make 2-3 slashes across
the top. Bake in the oven for 20-25
minutes until base sounds hollow
when tapped. Allow to cool on a
wire rack. Serve sliced and buttered
with cheese or plain with soup or
pasta.

Serves 6-8.

PIZZA LOAF

1 quantity Deep Pan Pizza Dough, made to end of step 1, see page 14

90 g (3 oz) sliced salami, chopped

3 spring onions, finely chopped

1 tablespoon chopped fresh herbs

TOPPING:

melted butter for brushing

4 slices processed Cheddar cheese

TOMATO AND BASIL BUTTER:

185 g (6 oz/¾ cup) butter, softened

3 teaspoons tomato purée (paste)

2 tablespoons finely chopped basil

1 teaspoon lemon juice

Grease a 500 g (1 lb) loaf tin. Knock back risen dough and knead dough with salami, spring onions and herbs. Shape to fit tin. Cover with plastic wrap and set aside until dough almost reaches top of tin.

Preheat oven to 190C (375F/Gas 5). Brush loaf with melted butter. Bake in the oven for 25-30 minutes until loaf sounds hollow when base is tapped. Turn out of tin and place on baking sheet. Slice cheese into strips and place in a lattice design over top. Return to oven and bake for 3-4 minutes to soften cheese a little. Cool.

Make Tomato and Basil Butter. In a bowl, beat butter with tomato purée (paste), basil and lemon juice. Spoon into dish and chill until required. Slice Pizza Loaf and serve with Tomato and Basil Butter.

Serves 6.

BREAD STICKS

1 quantity Traditional Pizza Dough, made up to end of step 2, see pages 10 and 11

sesame or poppy seeds, or cracked or kibbled wheat, to sprinkle

TO SERVE:

slices of prosciutto (Parma ham), if desired

Preheat oven to 200C (400F/Gas 6). Grease several baking sheets.

Knock back risen dough and knead briefly. Divide dough into approximately 18 equal-sized pieces and roll each piece to a 20 cm (8 in) length. Arrange on baking sheets and brush with water.

Leave plain or sprinkle with sesame or poppy seeds, or cracked or kibbled wheat, if desired. Bake in the oven for 15-20 minutes until crisp and golden. Allow to cool before serving plain or wrapped with slices of prosciutto (Parma ham), if desired, to serve as a cocktail snack.

Makes about 18.

POLENTA BREAD

220 g (7 oz/1⅓ cups) coarse ground cornmeal

125 g (4 oz/1 cup) plain flour

1 heaped teaspoon salt

¼ teaspoon black pepper

3 tablespoons olive oil

220 ml (7 fl oz/1 cup) hand-hot water

TO SERVE:

salad

Preheat oven to 220C (425F/Gas 7). Grease a 30 cm (12 in) pizza tin.

In a bowl, mix together the corn-meal and flour and season with salt and pepper. In a jug, whisk together 2 tablespoons oil and hand-hot water. Stir into the flour and mix with a fork to form a grainy paste.

Place in centre of tin and press to edges with the knuckles. Prick with a fork and brush with remaining oil. Bake in the oven for 20 minutes until golden. Serve the bread warm with salad.

Serves 4-6.

FOCACCIA

1 quantity Traditional Pizza Dough, made up to end of step 2, see pages 10 and 11

1 teaspoon crushed dried rosemary

about 18 stoned green olives

coarse sea salt, to sprinkle

rosemary sprigs, to garnish

Preheat oven to 220C (425F/Gas 7). Grease a 30 cm (12 in) pizza tin. Knock back risen dough and knead dough with crushed rosemary. Place dough in centre of tin and press to edges with knuckles. Prick all over with a fork. Press olives into dough. Brush with water and sprinkle with sea salt. Bake in the oven for 20 minutes until crisp and golden, Serve garnished with rosemary.

Serves 4-6.

Variations: Omit green olives and instead knead chopped black olives into dough with rosemary.

Or knead 60 g (2 oz/½ cup) freshly grated Parmesan cheese into dough and season to taste with a little black pepper. In both cases, prick dough with a fork, brush with water and, if desired, sprinkle with sea salt before cooking.

PIADINA

345 g (11 oz/2½ cups) strong white plain flour
1 heaped teaspoon salt
½ teaspoon baking powder
75 ml (2½ fl oz/⅓ cup) milk
3 tablespoons olive oil
TO SERVE:
salami, cheese and salad

In a bowl, mix flour with salt and baking powder. Mix milk with 75 ml (2½ fl oz/⅓ cup) water. Add oil and a little of the water and milk mixture to flour mixture. Stir with a fork and gradually add more liquid until it has all been incorporated. Mix to form a soft dough.

Turn onto a lightly floured surface and knead until smooth. Allow to rest for 15 minutes. Divide dough into 12 equal pieces. Roll each piece out to a circle measuring 7.5 cm (3 in) in diameter.

Heat a heavy-based frying pan or griddle until a drop of water flicked on the surface bounces and evaporates. Place 2-3 circles in pan or on griddle and cook for 30 seconds. Flip over and continue cooking.

Turn each circle 2 or 3 times until sides are speckled with brown. Place on wire rack while cooking remainder. Serve warm with salami, cheese and salad.

Serves 4-6.

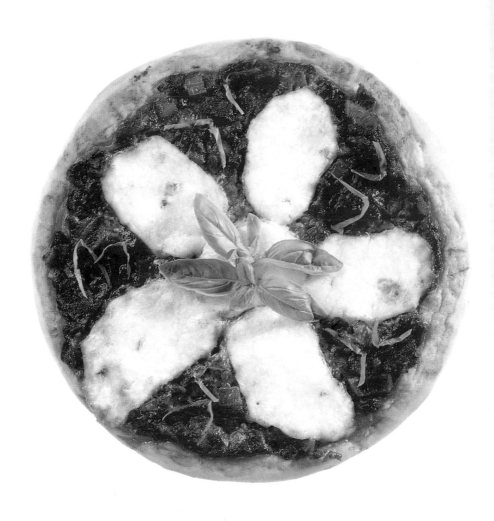

Pizza Margherita, page 19

Left:

Pizza Canapés, page 50
Ham & Tomato Bites, page 44

Centre:

Pesto Pizzelle, page 45

Right:

Pizza Canapés, page 50
Mozzolive Bites, page 53

Mexican Chilli Pizza, page 76

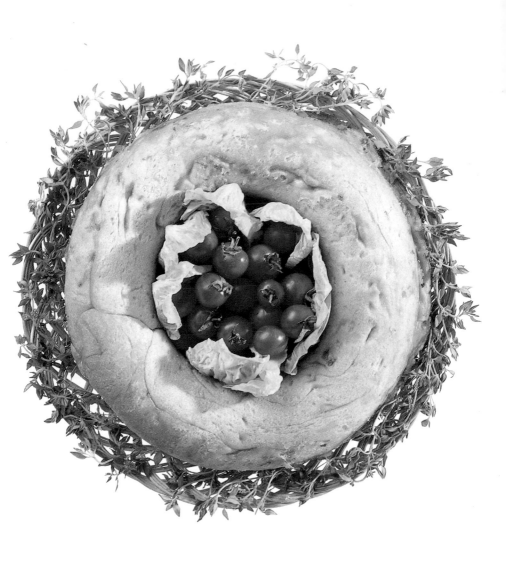

Pizza Ring, page 88

Orange Liqueur Pizza, page 104

Clockwise from top:

Walnut Bread, page 108
Polenta Bread, page 111
Bread Sticks, page 110
Piadina, page 113
Focaccia, page 112
Grape Bread, page 107
Panettone, page 106

Centre:

Pizza Loaf, page 109

INDEX